Nature Walks Around Victoria

Helen Lansdowne

NATURE WALKS *Around Victoria*

GREYSTONE BOOKS
Douglas & McIntyre Publishing Group
VANCOUVER/TORONTO

99 00 01 02 03 5 4 3 2 1

Greystone Books
A division of Douglas & McIntyre Ltd.
2323 Quebec Street, Suite 201
Vancouver, British Columbia V5T 4S7

Canadian Cataloguing in Publication Data

Lansdowne, Helen, 1958–
Nature walks around Victoria

ISBN 1-55054-702-X

1. Nature trails–British Columbia–Victoria Metropolitan Area–Guidebooks. 2. Natural history–British Columbia–Victoria Metropolitan Area–Guidebooks 3. Victoria Metropolitan Area (B.C.)–Guidebooks I. Title.
QH106.2.B7L36 1999 917.11'28044 C99-910042-4

Editing by John Eerkes
Front cover illustration by Fenwick Lansdowne
Interior photographs by Helen Lansdowne
Illustrations by Fenwick Lansdowne
Cover and text design by Peter Cocking
Typesetting by Susanna Gilbert, *Descriptions Design*
Printed and bound in Canada by Friesens
Printed on acid-free paper ∞

The publisher gratefully acknowledges the assistance of the Canada Council for the Arts and of the British Columbia Ministry of Tourism, Small Business and Culture. The publisher also acknowledges the financial support of the Government of Canada through the Book Publishing Industry Development Program for its publishing activities.

Contents

Introduction

THIS BOOK IS A guide to twenty-five walks in natural settings within a 40-km (25-mile) radius of downtown Victoria. These walks are designed for the novice, and most are short, under 2 km (1¼ miles) long. I have, however, included several more challenging walks, up to 8 km (5 miles) long. The chapters of this book are arranged geographically, from downtown Victoria north up the Saanich Peninsula and then west to Sooke. They are intended as a basic guide both to the parks themselves and to the many interesting and unusual sights to be seen on the trails. Although I frequently mention mammals, birds and insects, I have concentrated on the plant world in the belief that you definitely will see plants while you are out walking. You may be lucky and spot a black-tailed deer or catch sight of a pileated woodpecker, but you will not be able to miss the giant conifers towering above you. Nor, if you look, will you fail to find the delicate twinflower on the forest floor.

Victoria lies on the southernmost tip of Vancouver Island and is surrounded on three sides by ocean. Its west coast is exposed to the full force of the ocean and experiences seemingly endless storms in winter that roll in from the Pacific. Here rocky headlands stretch out into the ocean, interrupting the vast shoreline. On the eastern side of Victoria the coast is gentler, with protected bays and inlets. Three mainland mountain ranges—the Olympic, Cascade and Coast mountains—border the region and on clear days can be seen from any of the hill walks described in this book. Behind the shoreline lie lakes, rivers and farmlands, which provide a diversity of terrains, habitats and landscapes. The climate of southern Vancouver Island may be described as Mediterranean, with heavy rainfall in winter and dry spells in summer. Temperatures do not range to extremes and provide favourable conditions for the temperate rain forest that clothes the land.

The twenty-five walks in this book offer something for everyone. Roche Cove and the Galloping Goose Trail will take you through a temperate rain forest, whereas at Upper Thetis Lake a beautiful freshwater lake provides a different experience. Christmas Hill Park offers a walk through a Garry oak ecosystem, a rare and quickly diminishing habitat found only in the Mediterranean climate enjoyed by Victoria. For a riverside or estuary walk, try Goldstream Provincial Park or Cuthbert Holmes Park. If you are a lover of wildflowers, almost all the walks in this book will give pleasure of a botanical kind.

DEFINITIONS OF WALKING LEVEL

Easy: no longer than a 2-km (1¼-mile) round trip, with gentle undulation and a clean, wide path.

Moderate: no longer than a 3-km (2-mile) round trip, with some ups and downs but a clean trail.

Difficult: a longer route, with more ups and downs and a trail that is narrow and could have protruding rocks and roots. These walks are definitely not for those who have not walked before, because they border on being hikes rather than gentle walks.

These classifications are a rough guide only. We all have our own ideas of what is an easy or difficult walk and may wish to judge for ourselves. If you are unsure of the level of difficulty that you can handle, then err on the easy side.

SAFETY TIPS

The walks in this book are not dangerous, and if you follow the cautions in each chapter and refer to the maps you should have no trouble. There are, however, a few safety tips that should be observed to avoid accidents.

Dress for the trail: If you are walking during the rainy season, make sure you wear waterproof clothing; always use sturdy walking shoes because it is easy to trip and sprain an ankle on even the most level of walks.

Plan ahead: Before setting out, tell someone of your plans.

Stay on the trail: If you are an inexperienced walker, do not wander from the main trail; it is easy to get lost in the woods. If you lose your bearings, go back to the last trail marker, and if you get truly lost, stay in one place. You will then be easier to find.

Be prepared for a weather change: If the weather becomes inclement and you are not dressed for the change, abandon your walk rather than persevere.

Be careful on bridges and boardwalks: These are potentially the most dangerous features of the walks, particularly in the wet season, when they become slippery. Use caution and proceed slowly, testing your footing as you walk.

Bring water: On longer walks, it is advisable to carry drinking water.

Be wary of larger animals: Several walks, such as Jocelyn Hill, are in areas where you may be sharing the surroundings with larger resident animals. Talk or carry a bell while walking so that you won't surprise them. If you see a cougar or bear, keep your distance and allow the animal room to move away without feeling threatened.

THE ETHICS OF NATURE WALKING

When you walk through the parks around Victoria, remember that you are sharing them with many other living things. Don't leave anything behind, don't pick any wildflowers or fungi and don't disturb any of the many creatures that inhabit the area. If you look under a rock on the beach in search of crabs, put the rock back where you found it, for it is undoubtedly the home of some small creature. When walking through a rain forest, do not stray off the path; many amphibians make their homes under decaying wood on the forest floor and may be trampled without your realizing it. If you are a dog walker, pick up after your dog and respect the rules of the various parks, especially during the nesting season, which is usually April through June.

A PHILOSOPHY OF NATURE WALKING

We live in a high-tech world where, ironically, labour-saving devices seem to have created a busier life, one in which free time is at a premium. Walking in nature is a powerful antidote to the anxieties and frustrations of our fast-paced lives. But to truly benefit from what nature has to offer, turn off your Walkman, take off your sunglasses and be prepared to walk at a gentler pace, without constant conversation. Take time to listen to the sounds of the forest or smell the scents of a shoreline.

A small pair of binoculars is indispensable when walking in the country. If you are a birder, a pair with a 6- or 8-power magnification is best, but any size will allow you to see things you might otherwise miss. Also, a pocket magnifying glass takes no space and will reveal the beauty and complexity of flowers and other things too small for ordinary notice.

You may find that walking in the forest or along an estuarine shore quickens your interest in the plants and animals mentioned in these pages. If that is the case, take with you one of the many guidebooks to the natural history of the region. Recognizing and being able to put a name to something is not only a very satisfying thing, it is the first step toward knowledge and appreciation.

USEFUL GUIDEBOOKS

Capital Regional District Parks. *Birds of Witty's Lagoon* (brochure).

Capital Regional District Parks. *Wildflowers of Mill Hill* (brochure).

Farrand, John, Jr. *Western Birds: An Audubon Handbook.* New York: McGraw-Hill, 1988.

Lyons, C.P., and Bill Merilees. *Trees, Shrubs and Flowers to Know in British Columbia and Washington.* Vancouver: Lone Pine Publishing, 1995.

National Audubon Society. *Familiar Mushrooms.* New York: Alfred A. Knopf, 1995.

Pojar, J., and A. MacKinnon, eds. *Plants of Coastal British Columbia, including Washington, Oregon and Alaska.* Vancouver: B.C. Ministry of Forests and Lone Pine Publishing, 1994.

Royal British Columbia Museum Handbook Series.

Westin, Jim, and David Sterling, eds. *The Naturalist's Guide to the Victoria Region.* Victoria: Victoria Natural History Society, 1986.

Key to Maps

- Road
- Park boundary
- Body of water
- Picnic area
- Viewpoint
- End of trail
- Parking
- Marsh
- River
- Trail
- Secondary trail
- Rock
- Public toilet
- Building
- Boat ramp
- Bird blind
- Trees

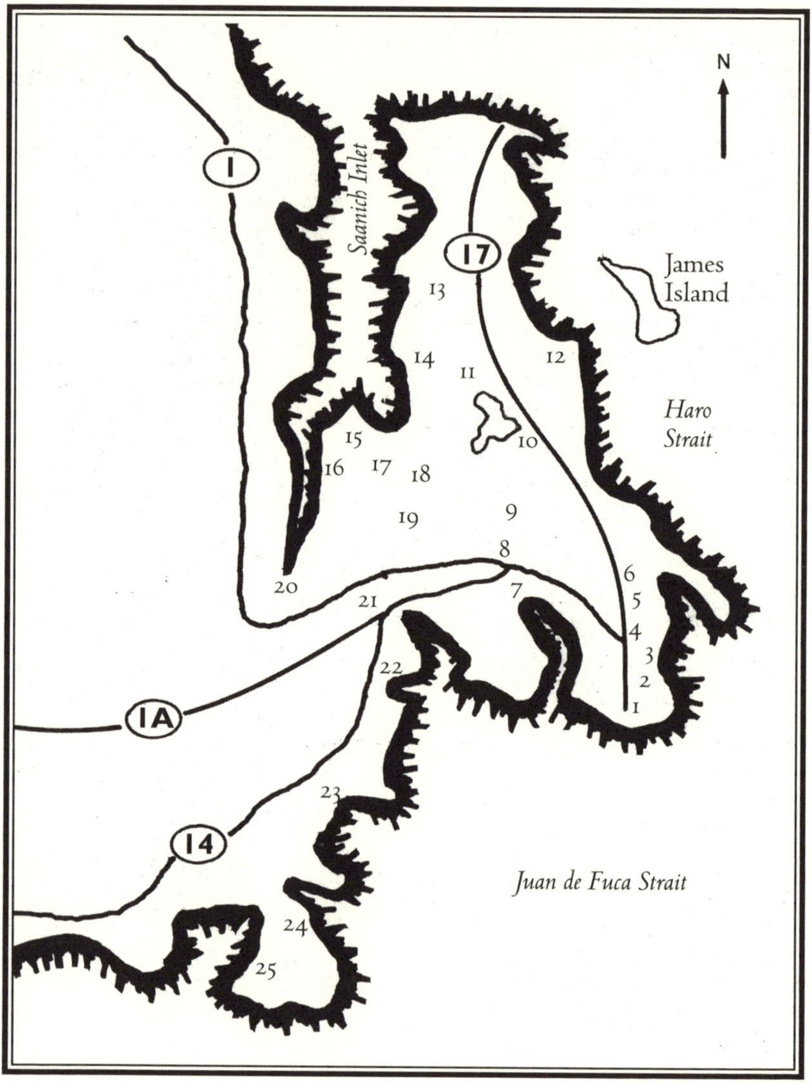

Victoria Area

Note: The maps in this book show the general locations of the featured parks, streets and trails. For detailed information, refer to Victoria-area street maps, CRD park maps and B.C. Parks park guides.

I

Beacon Hill Park

VICTORIA

HIGHLIGHTS: Heronry, waterfowl, Garry oaks, camas, pond lilies, Mayor's Grove

WALKING LEVEL: Easy

SEASON: All year

ATTIRE: Rainwear in winter

DOG WALKING: Excellent

ROUND TRIP: 2 km (1¼ miles)

BEACON HILL PARK IS surely one of Victoria's great institutions. Not only does it reflect the city's long tradition of gardening, but it preserves, albeit in microcosm, much of the native habitat that is a signature of the area. Set aside in 1858 by James Douglas, governor of the Vancouver Island colony, this 77-ha (200-acre) parcel of land became the city's park in 1882, when the province of British Columbia gave it in trust to the citizens of Victoria. Seven years later the city's ratepayers approved a loan bylaw of $25,000, a substantial sum for the time, to landscape the park. Although the well-maintained grounds are quite extensive and well worth seeing, the walk described in this chapter winds, for the most part, through the park's natural areas.

From the small parking lot on the south side of Southgate Street between Quadra and Douglas streets, follow the sidewalk for about 100 m (330 feet) toward Douglas. A paved path leads south into the park. For approximately 300 m (1000 feet), this paved path winds through a rocky area with scattered pines and stands of Garry oak. Although considerable areas of natural land remain in Beacon Hill, a number of unusual and beautiful exotic trees grow here as well. They have been brought from

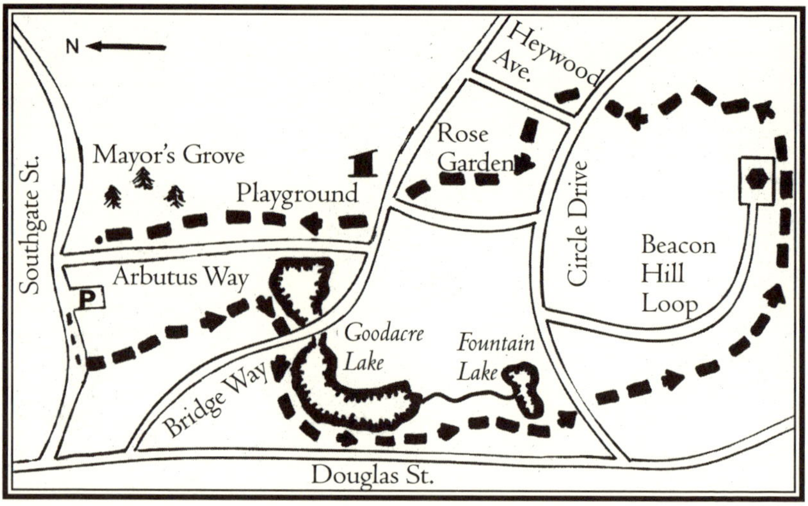

many different parts of the world, and their presence adds historical as well as visual interest to their surroundings. As you walk the trail now, look to your right for a view of a beautiful snow gum tree, which is rare in British Columbia. Although this tree is not part of our local flora—it is a native of Australia—its size and growth habit are well worth noting.

Continuing along the trail you reach the end of the native Garry oak habitat and enter the cultivated part of the park, designed and laid out by John Blair, a renowned Scottish landscape gardener. Under his supervision Goodacre and Fountain Lakes were constructed to provide a focal point to the gardens, and local residents contributed more than two thousand shrubs and trees to the grounds. Acorns from the native Garry oaks were planted on the hill and on bare areas throughout the park. Today, many of these native and non-native trees, now mature, grace the gardens and may be seen on this walk.

Upon approaching Goodacre Lake, look to your left for a view of three giant sequoias and a lovely English yew. The latter species is a tree of fabled longevity, so the example in Beacon Hill, though perhaps 100 years old, can be considered no more than youthful. To the left and behind the lake is a wonderful alpine and rock garden, planted and maintained by the Victoria Rock and Alpine Society. This little garden is well worth a detour, because there usually is something in bloom during most of the year.

At Goodacre Lake the path divides; take the right side and travel toward the far end of the lake. Wood ducks are sometimes on the water, but the variety of ducks seen here in winter has sadly declined in recent years. Although the canvasbacks and greater scaups of earlier times may come no more, hooded mergansers, shovellers, teals and the odd pintail make up for their absence. Keep an eye open, too, for the year-round resident population of painted turtles and Canada geese. Do not cross the stone bridge for the moment but continue down the path that runs parallel with the lake. It will lead you to the far side of Goodacre Lake, where it passes under an arbour overgrown with climbing roses and twisted stems of an ancient wisteria.

Walk quietly in this section; you are very near an active heronry. At the end of the arbour look to your right, where about 25 m (80 feet) up in a copse of Douglas-firs a number of untidy stick nests have been built. If you are here on a summer evening, the squawking and chattering of the herons as they arrive one by one and settle down to roost will undoubtedly catch your attention, for the noise is considerable. It is remarkable that a colony of these stately and magnificent birds can flourish in a city park, beside a busy road, when other more remote heronries have been abandoned because of the proximity of people. Their presence here is more interesting still when one realizes that not 100 m (300 feet) away, toward the seashore, is the active nest of a pair of bald eagles.

The path now travels away from the lake and passes through a stand of western red cedars and large Douglas-firs. You now travel alongside the stream that feeds into Goodacre Lake from Fountain Lake. Eventually the path crosses a bridge and brings you to Fountain Lake. This small body of water is a mass of yellow pond lilies, the only species of pond lily native to Victoria, and in midsummer the surface of the lake is a carpet of cup-shaped blooms.

Follow the right-hand path around the lake, and cross another two bridges. To your right, weeping birches and willows cascade over the water's edge. These are water-loving trees that do extremely well at the lakeshore. The path divides about 25 m (80 feet) from the last bridge; bear left here because the right-hand branch leads out of the park. You will come to still another division a short way along; once again, stay to the left, continuing around Fountain Lake to its far side. Before leaving the

Great blue heron by Goodacre Lake

lake, look for a European fan palm from North Africa, growing just behind the large clump of Portuguese laurel. The trail forks again near this point, and the route takes you away from the lake. On the left side of the path is an incense cedar, from southern Oregon. At first glance this tree closely resembles the native western red cedar, but look at a seed cone and count the scales. The incense cedar has six scales, whereas the western red cedar has eight to twelve.

After passing the incense cedar, walk across Circle Drive onto the road that leads up the hill. Look for a path, really no more than a track, on the left-hand side at the gates. This path crosses a large meadow bordered with shore pines and Garry oaks. In spring the meadow is ablaze with the blues and yellows of the countless blooms of camas and buttercup. The camas is the showiest and most lovely flower of the plants associated with the Garry oaks. To the resident Salish people, it had value beyond beauty. The camas bulb was an important staple food, and a meadow such as this would have attracted many harvesters. The Vancouver Island Coast Salish even semi-cultivated the bulb, growing camas beds that were owned and inherited.

The meadow leads to the top of Beacon Hill, named after a pair of masts that were intended as a navigational aid for mariners. The masts forming the "beacon" were lined up with a buoy offshore on Brotchie Ledge. Looking out on a clear day, you can enjoy a view of the Olympic Mountains across Juan de Fuca Strait and the constantly changing effects of light and atmosphere, which make the mountains seem different each time you see them. To your right is the Race Rocks lighthouse, one of the few still-manned lights on the coast. If it is spring, the slope below you on Beacon Hill will be a carpet of yellow provided by the thousands of daffodils that have naturalized here over the years.

Continuing on the route look for a grass trail leading down the hill east of the building, but before descending notice the dilapidated state of the building on the hilltop. For much of its life, this was an attractive, glassed-in lookout, where pensioners played shuffleboard, chatted and enjoyed viewing the passing ships. Time and vandalism have put an end to that. The downhill path winds through a thicket of Garry oaks and snowberry to the far side of the petting zoo. Cross Circle Drive and walk through the rose garden on the left side of Heywood Avenue. Proceed either along Heywood or along a paved path located 50 m (150 feet) from the rose garden.

You are now heading toward the Mayor's Grove, a good spot for a family outing. There are picnic tables nearby, and the grove provides a wonderful opportunity for children and adults to have some fun. On the south side of the grove is a board listing all the dignitaries who have commemorated their visit to Victoria by planting one of the many trees in the grove over the past century. Each tree has a headstone with a number corresponding to one on that board. See who can find the English hawthorn planted by Winston Churchill or the Douglas-fir planted in memory of David Douglas.

A number of native trees, including Garry oaks, Douglas-firs, and bigleaf maples, were planted in the grove. The exotic trees include ash, beech, copper beech, linden and hawthorn. All the trees are beautiful specimens that have grown and spread without hindrance in their spacious surroundings.

Common camas

At the north end of Mayor's Grove is the intersection of Southgate Street and Arbutus Way, from where it is only a short walk back to the parking lot.

HOW TO GET THERE: Drive along Douglas Street to Southgate Road. Turn east onto Southgate and watch for the small parking lot on the right-hand side of the road. If this lot is full, continue one block to Arbutus Way, turn right and park there.

2

Mount Tolmie Park

SAANICH

HIGHLIGHTS: Garry oaks, rock striations, camas, alligator lizards, vistas

WALKING LEVEL: Easy

SEASON: Spring

ATTIRE: Rainwear in wet months

DOG WALKING: Excellent

ROUND TRIP: 1 km (½ mile)

"THERE ARE FAIRIES IN the glen," my grandfather used to say to me as I walked with him through Mount Tolmie as a young child. Fairies? Perhaps not, but other equally delightful things exist in this Saanich park. Mount Tolmie stands in the centre of Victoria and provides magnificent 360-degree views of the surrounding areas.

Beside the parking lots at the top of Mount Tolmie you will see a large rock face with prominent parallel furrows or striations. Gouged into the surface of the bedrock during the last glaciation, they are a testimony to the tremendous weight and pressure of the ice as it carried its cargo of rock-scouring boulders seaward. Mount Tolmie is a monadnock—a steep-sided hill resistant to erosion—and it stands isolated, a blunt tower of rock. Look northeast from the top of Mount Tolmie and you will see Mount Douglas, another monadnock. Between the two prominences the land is flat, having been created by the sand and sediment that were swept along and deposited by the great ice sheets that scraped clean the monadnocks. All over Mount Tolmie, bare rock faces remind us of Victoria's geological past.

The trail starts just south of the reservoir beside the parking lot, where you walk down a flight of stone steps ending at a bark-mulch path.

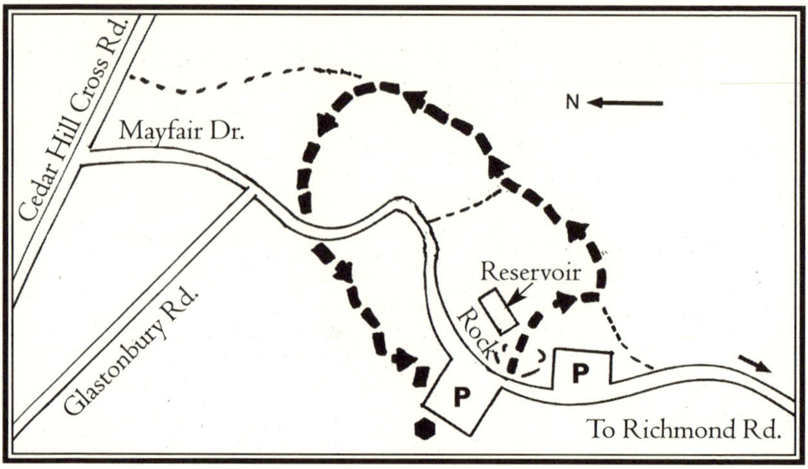

This winds through Garry oak and scrubland habitat and forks after about 50 m (165 feet). The left side leads to Mayfair Drive, so keep to the right-hand path. The route is lined with ocean spray, Himalayan blackberry and snowberry. A canopy of oaks, firs and arbutus keeps this section of the path shady, and within about 100 m (330 feet) the path divides again. Once more, take the trail to the right, and right again at the next division, 100 m (330 feet) further on. Soon after this last fork, the bark-mulch trail meets a paved fire road, which you follow. When the bark-mulch trail resumes soon after, look to the road and enjoy the sight of a large arbutus, which, having found enough space to spread, is a beautiful, expansive umbrella of red-brown limbs.

As you continue down the hill, you will notice that the shrubs and trees begin to thin out. The soil is shallow here, and there is more exposed rock. The oaks now grow singly, stunted and contorted by the dry heat of summer and the cold winds of winter. Extensive carpets of camas can be found in this area of the park during April and May. As a young child I was often taken to see the sweeping blanket of blue that covered the hillside. In recent years, the alien Scotch broom has threatened to push out the camas, as well as other plants such as satin flowers and fawn lilies.

Scotch broom was first introduced to Sooke in 1849 by Captain Walter Colquhoun Grant, a Scots settler who managed to establish three spindly seedlings before selling his property four years later. The invasive plant spread quickly and soon became a scourge throughout the region. The mild climate of the West Coast provides perfect growing conditions for broom, and its wiry branches, with their rich golden-yellow flowers, may reach its 4 m (13 feet) in height. Fortunately, through the efforts of local volunteers, the broom on this side of Mount Tolmie has been kept under control, allowing the camas to flourish once again. Another native plant, fireweed, has started to fill the gaps left by the eradicated broom. Look for its flaming pink flowers in the cleared areas during July and August and the accompanying buzz of honey bees, which are attracted to its sweet nectar.

Bees are not the only insects you will encounter while walking. One hot day in July, I walked this trail and was entertained by a chorus of cicadas. There are three cicada species native to Victoria. The most common, the western cicada, like all cicadas starts its life cycle with an egg laid on a twig high above the ground. Upon hatching, the immature cicada falls to earth and tunnels into the earth, where it feeds on the juice of roots for several years. Eventually, though, the young, wingless cicada crawls out of the ground and climbs a nearby tree. In a short time its outer skin splits behind its head, and the adult cicada emerges. If it is a male, it starts to "sing" to attract a female.

The lifespan of the adult cicada is short, perhaps only a few weeks, just enough time to attract a mate and for the female to lay an egg. Not all species of cicadas hatch at the same time, so their chorus of mating calls can last all summer.

As you travel downward, the trail turns to gravel and the path becomes steep. There is nothing on the trail to trip an unsuspecting walker, but the steepness of the terrain demands caution. This section of the trail is not long and soon becomes a gentle slope, once again becoming a bark-mulch trail.

Approximately 150 m (500 feet) from the end of the fire road, you will come to a divide in the trail. Bear left here and head toward the road. When you reach it you should be at the intersection of Glastonbury Road and Iona Place. Look for the "Walker" signpost at the trail entrance. Cross the road and pick up the bark-mulch trail on the other side; this path leads back up the mountain and eventually to the parking lot. Unfortunately, this part of the park has not received the attention given to the other side, and Scotch broom has invaded the whole area. The two

Footpath on Mount Tolmie

sections of the trail provide a useful comparison: the first side shows signs of rejuvenation, the other shows what happens when indigenous species are pushed out by a vigorous exotic plant.

About 200 m (650 feet) up the trail, the path opens out to a beautiful grassy clearing with picnic tables and lovely views eastward at the far side of the opening. This flat area bordered by Garry oaks makes a beautiful spot to stop and rest before heading up the last section of the walk. When you leave the clearing the path winds through a particularly dry section, a habitat for northern alligator lizards. Although you might think that such a creature, with a body from 17 to 23 cm (7 to 9 inches) long, would be easily visible, it is not. Alligator lizards are brownish grey, the colour of the surrounding rocks, and are able to blend perfectly into their surroundings. If you are lucky enough to spot one basking in the sunshine or scuttling through the undergrowth, move slowly or the lizard will dart for cover.

The trail continues to wind its way back up Mount Tolmie through an exposed area that, in summer, is the hottest part of the park. If it is suitable here for lizards, it is also hot and dry enough to attract an occasional lazuli bunting, the brilliant blue-and-chestnut finch usually more at home in the southern interior of the province. Take time to stop and rest on a bench that can be found halfway up the mountain, under the shade of the oak trees. Although there are many subsidiary paths in this part of the park, stay on the main bark-mulch trail. About 150 m (500 feet) from the clearing, the trail ends at an open gravel wasteland. Continue up the mountain along the edge of Mayfair Drive for about 100 m (330 feet), and you will reach the parking lot.

HOW TO GET THERE: From Richmond Road between Hillside Avenue and Cedar Hill Cross Road, turn east onto Mayfair Drive. Or, from Cedar Hill Cross Road between Richmond Road and Gordon Head Road, turn south onto Mayfair Drive. Mayfair Drive runs through the park and will take you to the parking lots at the summit of Mount Tolmie.

3

Uplands Park

OAK BAY

HIGHLIGHTS: Garry oaks, camas, satin flowers, butterflies, birdwatching

WALKING LEVEL: Easy

SEASON: Mid to late spring

ATTIRE: Waterproof shoes in winter

DOG WALKING: Excellent, but not allowed during bird-nesting season, March–May

ROUND TRIP: 1.5 km (1 mile)

FOR VISITORS AND LOCAL residents who want to walk in a natural area close to the city, Uplands Park is the first choice. It is one of the largest and richest natural areas left in the region and may easily be reached by bus or car from the downtown core. This 30-ha (76-acre) park in the heart of Oak Bay provides easy and beautiful walks through a largely unspoiled Garry oak woodland. Designated as parkland in 1946, Uplands has preserved not only a considerable Garry oak meadow and woodland with a wide range of native plants but also a rocky beach known as Cattle Point, much used by dog walkers and seagull feeders.

All the main paths on the west side lead into the heart of the park, but walkers should be forewarned that in winter, spring and autumn the paths are extremely wet and muddy. Although this renders them disagreeable underfoot, wetness has its pleasures; a snipe may burst from the boggy ground at one's feet and jink swiftly away on pointed wings. All four entrances on the west side lead through open, grassy areas with Garry oaks, red alders and bitter cherry. Within 100 m (300 feet), the grass gives way to dense hedgerows of wild roses, Indian plum and snowberries intertwined with blackberry brambles and both orange-flowering and purple-

Garry oaks in Uplands Park

flowering honeysuckles. These honeysuckles are native to the coast. The showier of the two is the orange, a vigorous, tree-twining species and a favourite with the rufous hummingbird. The other, with a more horizontal growth habit, tends to ramble over stumps and fences. Its small, wine-purple blossoms are easily overlooked.

It is in the hedgerows where most of the park's birds will be found. Towhees with handsome chestnut sides and black, white-spotted, upper parts keep close to the ground, skulking in the shrubbery they share with chocolatey, melodious song sparrows. Bolder species like chestnut-backed chickadees can usually be found somewhere in the park, as can the stripy, red-fronted house finches, whose sweet warble may be heard on sunny days in late winter. Parties of bushtits, grey, tiny and feather-light, may be seen working the hedgerows. In March, watch for their hanging nests, beautifully woven of plant down and lichen and suspended from slender branches in the shrubbery, a little above head height.

Springtime arrivals include orange-crowned warblers, whose simple trill is a characteristic sound of spring, and a couple of weeks later, the brighter yellow Wilson's warblers, with their neat, black caps. At any time of year there are flickers, downy woodpeckers and California quail. More sinister residents also may be glimpsed from time to time; they include Cooper's hawks and an occasional great horned owl or barred owl.

Although the park's trails do not extend much more than a kilometre in any given direction, the richness of its flora makes for an appealing walk. The most spectacular walk in the park begins at the entrance on Beach Drive, approximately 10 m (33 feet) east of the start of the Cattle Point scenic loop, where there is ample parking for cars.

Walking into the park, you are met by stands of large Garry oaks. These are not the spindly trees found in drier areas of Victoria or the stunted, wind-clipped specimens that cling to Cattle Point shore a few hundred metres away. They are truly giants of their kind, growing in an open, natural parkland of great beauty. Following the main path, you soon come to a fork. Try the left branch, which ascends and passes over a rocky outcrop and then through a woodland where, in late March and early April, shooting stars and fawn lilies bloom profusely.

Throughout Uplands Park the walking is easy, though somewhat soggy in the winter months. Unfortunately, much of the park has been infiltrated by Scotch broom, an invasive plant that arrived with an early settler and has since crowded out many indigenous species. Community efforts to eradicate this species are under way, and volunteer work parties may sometimes be seen industriously cutting and pulling up the tenacious clumps.

Following along, the trail runs parallel with Beach Drive and opens onto another rocky shelf. It is here that one of our most attractive wildflowers, the satin flower, can be found in early spring. This little plant, with its single, fuschia pink bells, should not be confused with the more prolific shooting star, whose stalk bears two or three flowers, also pink, with sharply swept-back petals. In late spring this same area is home to

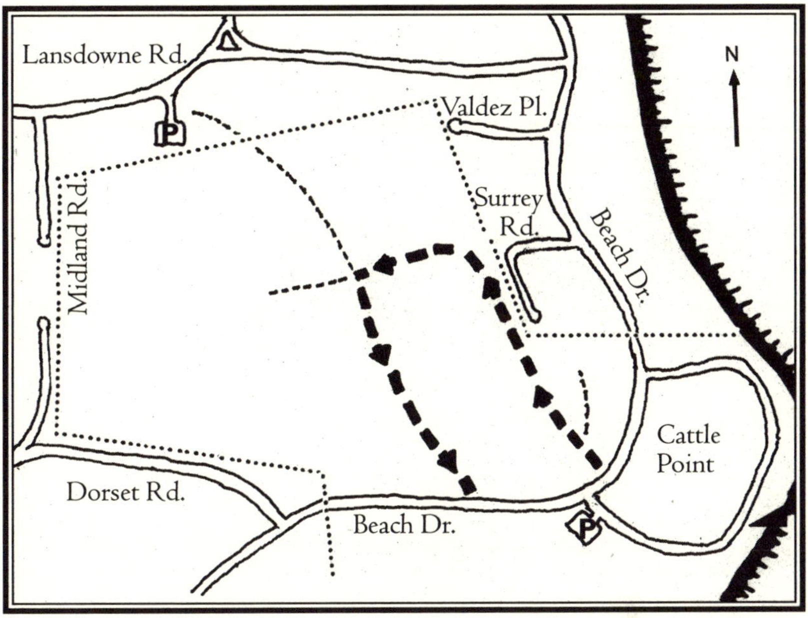

the true treasure of Uplands Park, the common camas. One might also be lucky and find the larger great camas; you can easily tell the two apart because the great camas never has more than three flowers open at one time. This lovely blue flowering plant, whose edible bulbs were harvested by the Salish people, blooms in profusion from early April to the beginning of May.

Late spring is the time of the park's greatest beauty, when the ground between the budding, widely spaced oaks is a violet blue carpet of camas punctuated by the magenta drifts of the last of the shooting stars and sprinkled with the yellow of spring gold. It is also the time of the year when several species of butterflies make their appearance. Among the first are fast-flying, rusty orange tortoiseshells, and tiny blues like specks of sky. Early April is the time to watch for yellow and black anise swallowtails, and May brings the bigger, more showy tiger swallowtails. In midsummer keep an eye open for the more leisurely Lorquin's admirals, gliding on black and white wings with orange corners. Until a few years ago the park was home to an unobtrusive little butterfly, the Edith chequerspot, which fluttered at grass-top height in camas time.

Shooting star

Unfortunately, some change in Victoria's conditions has tipped the scales, and it has vanished from this and most of its former haunts.

The rocky path gives way once again to woodland, where hedgerows of wild rose and snowberries line the paths. Approximately 100 m (300 feet) farther along, the path opens onto the central meadow, the heart of the park. This area is rich in native plants, including many types of grasses and herbs, and provides a breathtaking view of the Garry oaks. For those who have a serious interest in botany, the Victoria Natural History Society has listed and plotted the location of all the native and exotic plants in Uplands Park. The number of species to be found is astonishing.

If you continue along the main path, your steps will take you back to Beach Drive. Look for the arbutus tree on the left, about 20 m (65 feet) before the end of the trail. This exceptionally large specimen, with its distinctive peeling red bark and leathery leaves, is one of the few of its kind in the park. Arbutus, also known as Pacific madrone, is a beautiful species and in Canada is unique to the drier, sunnier parts of southern Vancouver Island and the Gulf Islands.

There are many variations on the circular walk described above for those who wish to depart from the main trail and take one of the many smaller paths toward the ocean. On the woodland edge, facing the sea and across the road (Beach Drive) from Cattle Point, you will come upon the Cenotaph or War Memorial, erected shortly after World War II, when Uplands Park was created. On the small, landscaped lawn before it, a Remembrance Day ceremony is held every year on November 11. Cross the road to Cattle Point, which offers lovely views of two wooded islands in the middle distance—Chatham and Discovery. These islands are named after the ships in Captain George Vancouver's expedition, and for as long as anyone can remember they have been the roosting place of Oak Bay's crows, who stream home every evening across the bay. The shoreline, rising to a low bluff with a growth of scrub oak on the right, is otherwise rocky and flat. In early years this feature made the shoreline a useful landing and loading place for cattle, hence the name Cattle Point.

The shore offers some interesting birdwatching, particularly in winter, when several species of ducks join other seabirds on the sheltered waters of the coast. Beautifully painted harlequin ducks feed along the shore, and the equally handsome hooded mergansers are also sometimes seen here, resting "at anchor," with their heads pulled in and tails cocked. Gulls of various species congregate here at any time, hoping for handouts. Most numerous are the glaucous-winged gulls, but herring, western and California gulls are also common. Standing beside the dumpy little black turnstones and other shorebirds like the dunlin that scuttle about the rocks or over the gravelly beach, they look enormous.

Also watch for the striking black oyster-catchers, with their huge scarlet bills and pink legs. Their shrill, whinnying cries always attract attention, although the birds are surprisingly inconspicuous when feeding. Just in case you have missed them, a small party will suddenly leap into flight, screaming wildly as they circle and twist over the bay. This endangered species nests on rocky shorelines, so keep your dog on a leash during the nesting season, from March to May.

HOW TO GET THERE: Uplands Park may be entered from a variety of points. The west side of the park, bordered by Midland Road, has two entrances, with two more off Dorset Road. Once in, you may take any of a number of paths to the middle of the park.

From Beach Drive, turn south onto the Cattle Point scenic loop. Parking is available just after the turnoff, and the walk starts immediately across Beach Drive.

4
Rithet's Bog

SAANICH

HIGHLIGHTS: Cattails, shore pines, birdwatching

WALKING LEVEL: Easy

SEASON: All year

ATTIRE: Warm and waterproof clothing in winter

DOG WALKING: Not allowed

ROUND TRIP: 1 km (½ mile)

OVER THE PAST TEN years, Victoria has grown by leaps and bounds, and much of the greenbelt that once surrounded the city has been transformed into residential subdivisions. The walk featured in this chapter lies in the middle of one such area, Broadmead. The developers of this subdivision, the Guinness family (suppliers of stout to the world) left a small pocket of low-lying natural habitat, known as Rithet's Bog, as protected land. Although now completely surrounded by housing estates, this sensitive wetland area provides a gem of a walk.

A bog provides habitat for a rich assortment of moisture-loving plants, amphibians and bird life. In a sense, it forms from the top down, as the site of a drying lake or pond becomes favourable for the emergence of specialized plants such as sphagnum moss, pitcher plants and sundews, as well as heathers, sedges and grasses. Because of the spongy sphagnum moss, Rithet's Bog is damp and springy underfoot; the ground quakes as you walk over the surface. Strictly speaking, most of this park is not bog but a marsh, "bog" being applicable only to the central "island," with its slightly sinister covering of dark shore pines.

From the parking lot, take the entrance down a gravel path, or enter the park from Dalewood Lane and walk downhill for 200 m (650 feet). Both entrances take you to the main trail, which winds around the circumference

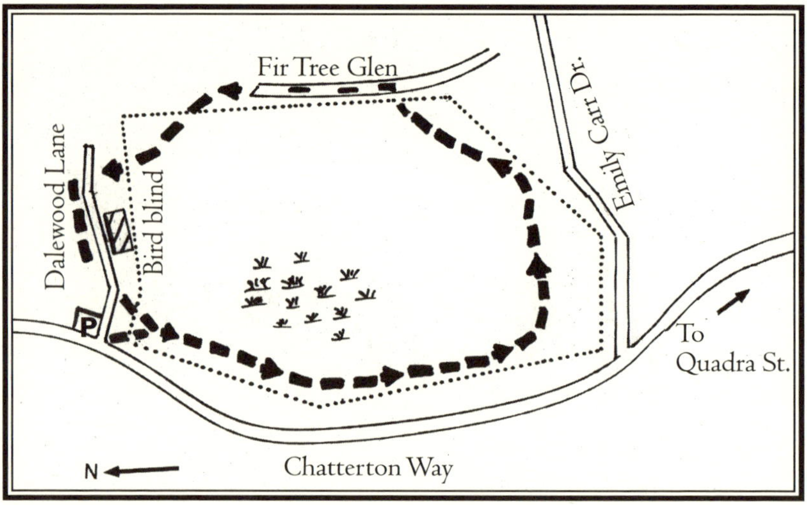

of the bog. The first part of the trail is bordered by a tangle of blackberries, poison hemlock and grasses interspersed with willows, hawthorns and hardhack. It's a treasure trove for tiger swallowtails. About 125 m (400 feet) from the start is a bench facing the lowest part of the marsh, in which water remains all year. Here in the breeding season you may see one or two mallards, single mothers, anxiously shepherding their broods of ducklings. Until they can fly at the end of the summer, the ducklings will feed and grow fat on the teeming aquatic life of the pond.

In duckling season, look for the bright yellow carpet of silverweed flowers and the red stems of the marsh cinquefoil in this low area. A characteristic plant growing in this part of the walk is the hardstemmed bulrush or tule, standing tall and firm with a paintbrush-like tip of brown fruit. The strength and thickness of the bulrush stalk made this plant an important mat-making material for Vancouver Island's Salish people.

About half a kilometre (⅓ mile) from the start of the trail, the path turns a right angle and no longer travels parallel to Chatterton Way. In a ditch running along the outside of the path you will find comfrey and mare's tails, while on the bog side grow stands of cattails. The cattails make an interesting show at any time of the year, either in the pale light of winter, when the old foliage is bleached and faded, or in summer, when the new flower spikes stand tall among the tattered, downy heads of the previous season. These dense, velvety flower heads carry both female flowers, on the main portion, and male flowers, on the cone-shaped top. As the male flowers break away and disperse, the tips of the stems are left bare while the chocolate-brown female flowers remain with their mustard-yellow pollen glinting in the sunlight.

Cattails furnish nesting habitat and building material for small animals and birds, some of which, like the marsh wren, are closely associated with this plant. Only in a cattail marsh will you hear, as you can at Rithet's Bog, the wren's buzzing, mechanical song, or see its active form, stripy and straw-coloured like the cattails themselves. Red-winged blackbirds, too, are primarily birds of the marsh. If you visit the park in summer, you will hear their song and see the flash of scarlet on black as the males display their plumage.

As you walk the trail, look across to the copse of cottonwood and hawthorn growing in the middle of the bog. Here, the next stage of land reclamation has brought more substantial plant species. This part of the path takes you past a large, low-lying rock face on the bog side of the trail. On the rock's surface grow lichens, rarely glanced at but interesting and curious combinations of algae and fungus. Producing an acid that eventually etches away the top layer of rock, they are an important element in soil production.

In the crevices of the rock, sheep sorrel and small-flowered forget-me-not thrive. Beyond the rock lie thickets of swamp laurel, black twinberry and purple flowering bittersweet. Farther down the path views of the bog become less frequent, obscured by the growth of cottonwoods, wild roses and red-osier dogwoods on the inner side of the trail. On this side, the nature sanctuary is bordered by a particularly obtrusive housing development.

If you walk the bog in early summer, enjoy the many varieties of native grasses that grow along the path. Yellow and pink seed heads gently fluttering in the breeze make a blanket of muted hues against a backdrop of shades of green. Both the dwarf and Nootka rose can be found here; they are easily distinguished by the size of their flowers and their peculiarity of growth. The Nootka rose grows to 3 m (10 feet), with showy flowers that are often 5 cm (2 inches) across. The flowers are often borne singly, but are sometimes in clusters of two or three. The dwarf rose

Common cattails at Rithet's Bog

grows only 1.2 m (4 feet) high. Its flowers are smaller, from 1 to 2 cm (½ to 1 inch) across, and are borne singly at the ends of twigs.

Look in the ditches that run along the outside of the path if you wish to find some of the wildlife of this area, particularly amphibians. The most numerous of these, the Pacific tree frog, makes its presence audible to all in March. Look for water striders, whose flat, pad-like feet support their bodies as they walk on the surface of the water. Also in the ditches grows common watercress, with its dark green foliage and bright white flowers. This plant was brought to North America by Europeans as a convenient food for early miners and settlers, but like so many alien species it has become naturalized over a wide range.

Just short of 2 km (1¼ miles) from its beginning, the trail ends at a paved road that winds through a residential area but on the perimeter of the bog. After about 300 m (1000 feet) leave the paved road, pick up another trail and cross a wooden bridge. Once it crosses the bridge, the trail forks. The left branch resumes the Rithet's Bog walk, and the other leads through Broadmead trail. As you walk, notice the change in vegetation. You have moved away from the bog and are in a drier region, a mixed forest of conifers and deciduous trees, Douglas-firs, red alders, arbutus and Garry oaks.

When passing the Garry oaks, take a moment to look at the underside of the leaves. The orange lumps under some leaves are signs of the gall wasp, a vigorous insect whose larvae feed on oak leaves. On windless summer nights, if you listen carefully, you can hear the gall wasps moving on the surface of the leaves. Not far from the end of the trail is a bench for resting, but better views are to be had from the benches and lookouts on Dalewood Lane. The trail ends on Dalewood, and from there a short walk leads back to the parking lot.

HOW TO GET THERE: Rithet's Bog is located off Dalewood Lane. From Highway 17, turn east onto Quadra Street. Once on Quadra, turn left (north) onto Chatterton Way. Travel up Chatterton Way, passing Emily Carr Drive. At the corner of Chatterton and Dalewood Lane, you will find the parking lot and trailhead.

5

Swan Lake Park

SWAN LAKE–CHRISTMAS HILL NATURE SANCTUARY SAANICH

HIGHLIGHTS: Waterfowl, painted turtles, floating bridge, heritage cottonwood trees

WALKING LEVEL: Easy; partially wheelchair accessible

SEASON: All year

ATTIRE: Rainwear in autumn and winter

DOG WALKING: Not allowed

ROUND TRIP: 2 km (1¼ miles)

NEW YORK BOASTS ITS red-tailed hawks breeding in downtown Manhattan, and Toronto has peregrine falcons that nest on its highrise buildings. Victoria has something equally remarkable, Swan Lake, a thriving nature sanctuary lying in the urban heartland. It is home to a wide variety of birds and animals, some of them transients passing through on migration and others that breed there and are part of the permanent population. The gentle walk around the lake allows people of all ages and abilities to view the wildlife and is especially recommended for families.

From the parking lot, take the bark-mulch trail to the nature house. If you have young children with you, spend a few minutes there before going on. The nature house has many touchable displays, which will give even very young children a good idea of what might be seen on the trail. Older people, too, can learn much to make their walk around the lake a richer experience.

From the nature house, walk down to the native plant garden, which is just before the floating bridge. This garden is full of indigenous plants, many of which have been rescued from certain destruction by development excavators.

Mallard on boardwalk at Swan Lake

The floating bridge you will reach shortly after leaving the nature house is a jetty and juts over the water, allowing visitors to sit and watch the activities of the lake. Swan Lake is a good example of a "eutrophic" body of water—it is rich in nutrients. Once a much larger and cleaner lake, it has been reduced in size and purity by organic runoff from surrounding farms, wineries and sewers, which has promoted the growth and encroachment of vegetation on the lake's perimeter. Today, the shallow waters of Swan Lake are filled with cattails and common duckweed, providing abundant food and refuge for several species of waterfowl.

The marshy habitat is particularly congenial to the dabblers of the duck family, and at any season you can be pretty sure of finding mallards and green-winged teals. Between breeding seasons they will be joined by American widgeons and a few of their chestnut-headed close cousins, Eurasian widgeons. Look also for the fish-eating ducks such as buffleheads, ring-necked ducks, lesser scaups and hooded mergansers. Often there are less frequently seen species here, too, like the shy soras and Virginia rails, peregrines and harriers. You may also see the dumpy and endearing coots, who paddle about on preposterous green feet, making noises like ancient bicycle horns.

When you leave the floating bridge, take the trail that leads to the right, a combination of loose gravel and intermittent boardwalks that make the walking easy and free from mud on even wet winter days. The boardwalks travel through thickets of willow submerged in stagnant water that is completely covered by duckweed and other aquatic plants.

Swan Lake is home to several semi-aquatic mammals, including the nocturnal raccoon. The rustling among the willow stems may be a foraging muskrat, a mink or even a river otter fishing in the shallows. Continue down the trail, and you will come to an open boardwalk across the lake. It puts you almost level with the water's surface, as if you were rafting across the lake. Painted turtles inhabit this area, and in summer they can be spotted on a log, basking in the sun, or prowling the water's edge in search of the perfect sandy pocket to lay their eggs. In winter, when the weather turns cold, the painted turtles bury themselves in the lake bottom.

Once across the boardwalk, you begin to move away from the lake on a gravel path through hedges of willow, hardhack and blackberry. This is a damp area, a reminder that the lake once extended much farther on this side. Now pioneer plants such as alder, hawthorn and reed canary grass have become well established. As you round a bend and walk parallel with the lake, look for a stand of giant cottonwoods. This copse of "heritage" trees contains some of the largest and oldest cottonwoods in the region. Tall hedgerows of maple, willow, bitter cherry and European bittersweet obscure any view of the lake, but a bench along the trail makes this is a good area to sit and watch for the wrens, warblers or any of the small songbirds that in one season or another populate the park.

The trail winds its way around the lake and through a much drier section, where Garry oaks and arbutus begin to appear among Douglas-firs. Rock outcroppings also begin to border the path, and the dank odours of the lake edge are replaced by the parched scent of oak leaves and arbutus bark. Ignore the many paths that lead away from the main trail; these are park exits leading to the surrounding residential areas.

At the far end of the lake is another floating bridge, which, like the first, invites a few moments' quiet contemplation by grown-ups. Children may prefer to lie on their tummies and look for sunfish or giant water beetles. The trail that continues around the lake from the second floating bridge becomes somewhat rougher, with protruding rocks and tree roots.

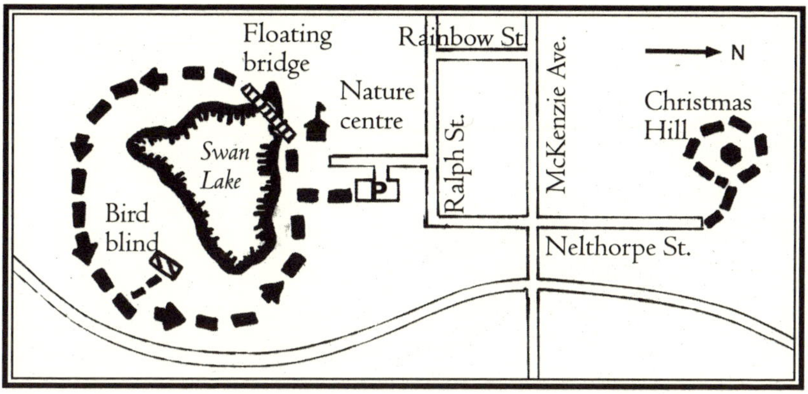

Those with limited mobility and those who are pushing baby strollers should turn back at this point.

Continuing around the lake, the trail passes through an eroded area where large rocks have slid down the bank. Note the sheltered eddy of water, cut off from the main lake, where aquatic vegetation is thick and rich and the surface teems with insects. Here a duck may be quietly paddling or a dragonfly swooping down to pluck a mosquito from the air. As you continue down the last section of the walk, the trail passes through a Garry oak woodland, where wildflowers bloom in the spring.

Keep your eyes open for the birds of prey that can sometimes be seen at Swan Lake. In addition to the peregrines and harriers that hunt over the marsh, Cooper's hawks and little sharp-shins terrorize the small birds and eagles terrorize the ducks. You may glimpse or even occasionally hear a great horned owl.

Just before you reach the parking lot, the trail passes by a side trail marked "Christmas Hill." If you wish a longer walk take this trail, which leads up to another nature sanctuary and is described in the next chapter. If you don't want to extend your expedition, the parking lot is only a short distance down the main trail.

HOW TO GET THERE: Swan Lake Park is located off Ralph Street. From Highway 17, turn east onto McKenzie Avenue and watch for Rainbow Street, 1 block east of the turnoff. Turn right onto Rainbow and then left onto Ralph Street. Swan Lake parking lot is at the end of Ralph.

Red-winged blackbird

6

Christmas Hill Park

SWAN LAKE–CHRISTMAS HILL NATURE SANCTUARY

SAANICH

HIGHLIGHTS: Garry oaks, wildflowers, rocky outcrops, butterflies, vistas

WALKING LEVEL: Moderate

SEASON: Spring

ATTIRE: Sturdy walking shoes

DOG WALKING: Not allowed

ROUND TRIP: 2.5 km (1½ miles)

IN THE EARLY 1980s Christmas Hill, an extensive tract of Garry oak habitat lying north of Swan Lake, came under the threat of urban development. Through the tireless efforts of local naturalists, this land was saved from the bulldozers and added to Swan Lake Nature Sanctuary. Whether you have walked the Swan Lake trail and wish to extend your journey or would simply like to explore a particularly lovely Garry oak ecosystem, Christmas Hill's walking trail is the place. This sanctuary offers woodland, parkland and scattered stands of Douglas-fir, as well as meadows and open rock.

If you are walking from the far end of the Swan Lake parking lot or from the Swan Lake trail, take the well-marked path running up to Nelthorpe Street. Cross McKenzie Avenue and pick up the trail on the north side, starting at the traffic lights. Passing through a residential area, the pathway is bordered by large Garry oaks and the familiar hawthorns and shrubs of snowberry laced and overgrown with blackberry.

The trail is a gentle uphill climb, crossing Lakeview Avenue 250 m (800 feet) along and continuing on the other side. Stone steps have been built into the trail where the grade is steeper, making it an easy walk.

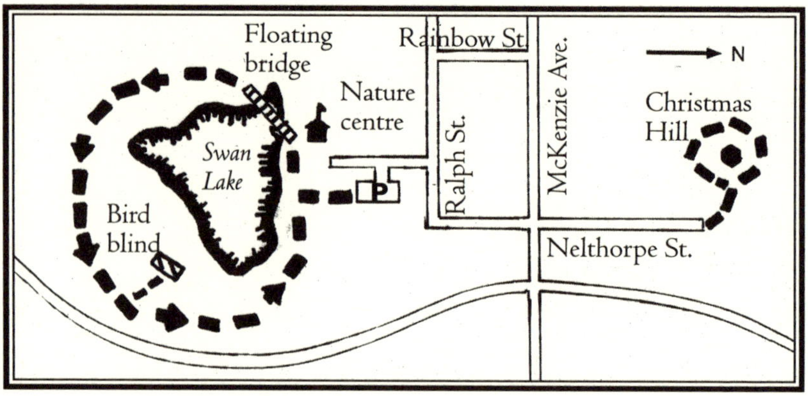

Soon you cross another paved road, Nicholson Street, and come to the beginning of Christmas Hill Park. Large, first-growth Douglas-firs standing among arbutus, grand firs and Garry oaks create a dry forest quite different from the damp cedar groves of the West Coast.

The trail continues to climb and passes through "parkland," an irregularly wooded landscape with open spaces where shrubs of ocean spray and snowberry thrive. Climb further and you reach a Garry oak meadow. Spring and early summer are the seasons of greatest beauty here; at these times bright wildflowers and lush grasses carpet the ground beneath the widely spaced trees. Blue camas, pink sea blush, white fawn lily and yellow western buttercup all contribute to the palette of colours that, set against the rich hues of the native grasses, is one of the chief delights of southern Vancouver Island.

Walking on, you come to the start of the summit, where the trail divides and forms a 500-m (1650-foot) circular route. Take the left-hand side and travel up about 25 m (80 feet) to reach a fork. The left-hand path leads to the top of a rock and a magnificent view of Swan Lake. Return to the main trail and travel west to a second rock lookout, this one facing central Saanich. The circle continues to the third and highest rock, which offers a 360-degree view of Victoria. From the top of Christmas Hill the views in any direction are very fine, and there are many good spots to sit and enjoy them.

The top of Christmas Hill is also a good place for butterflies. Each has its season; the first warm spring days bring tiny blues, followed by

Entrance to Christmas Hill Nature Sanctuary

orange-tips, anise swallowtails and, a little later, ringlets, meadow crescents and fast-flying skippers. Tiger swallowtails, so noticeable in early summer, are succeeded by stately, soberly coloured Lorquin's admirals. As the days grow hotter, giddy painted ladies in tawny orange and black sun themselves on warm rocks, joined occasionally by handsome red admirals.

The rocky outcrops are also the place to watch for garter snakes or alligator lizards basking in the sun. Also remember to look up. There may be a red-tailed hawk or other bird of prey soaring in lazy spirals above you. If you are here or anywhere in the Victoria area in the last week of September, you may be lucky enough to see one of the great flocks of migrating turkey vultures, which pass by on their way to California. It is an impressive sight; thirty, fifty or a hundred great black shapes wheeling slowly around the sky in absolute silence.

Continue down the final stage of the summit back to the marker, from where you can retrace your steps to McKenzie Avenue and then to the Swan Lake parking lot.

HOW TO GET THERE: Christmas Hill Park can be approached from the Swan Lake parking lot. From Highway 17, turn east onto McKenzie Avenue. From McKenzie, turn right onto Rainbow Street. Then turn left onto Ralph Street, and continue to the end of the street to the parking lot.

7
Cuthbert Holmes Park

SAANICH

HIGHLIGHTS: Estuary, creek, birdwatching, wildflowers, picnic area

WALKING LEVEL: Easy; wheelchair accessible

SEASON: All year

ATTIRE: Rainwear during wet weather

DOG WALKING: Excellent

ROUND TRIP: 2.2 km (1¼ miles)

FOR WHEELCHAIR USERS AND those wishing a gentle stroll through a largely natural landscape, one of the most accessible walks near Victoria is Cuthbert Holmes Park. Named in honour of Major H. Cuthbert Holmes, a leading advocate of preserving greenbelt land along the Colquitz River, this park is a testament to the foresight of its namesake. Bordered on one side by a highway and on the other by intensive residential development, this 27-ha (68-acre) park includes four different habitat zones, including estuary, hedgerow and disused field, mixed woodland and coniferous forest.

A paved path through the middle of the park makes an interesting and beautiful walk through a mixture of deciduous trees and conifers and out onto meadowland, but this chapter focuses on an alternative bark-mulch trail. This trail takes walkers to the edge of an estuary and through an abandoned heron rookery before it rejoins the paved trail. Taking this route will enable you to experience all four habitat zones.

From the Admirals Road entrance, start on the paved walk but look for the bark-mulch trail approximately 30 m (100 feet) along and to your right. The beginning of this trail takes one through a patch of mixed forest with an understorey of snowberry bushes and blackberry vines.

Colquitz Creek

Approximately 70 m (230 feet) from the start of the bark-mulch trail is a clearing, where you will see buttercups and wild roses as well as native grasses such as the common velvet grass. This part of the park was once farmland; looking at it, you can clearly see the progress of the plant succession that occurs once farming ceases and the land slowly returns to its original state. Already the grasses and wildflowers are being overcome by small shrubs like wild roses, while in the middle distance grow their successors, the hawthorns.

Beyond the shrubbery, a stand of Douglas-firs marks the final stage of the change. In time, if it is left undisturbed, a mature forest will replace the present meadow. A grassy path leads through the meadow to a picnic table and bench. If the weather is fine, sit here quietly for a few minutes and watch. It is surprising what you may see as, your presence forgotten, the natural life of the park resumes.

After about 70 m (230 feet) the trail branches. Take the right side and at the next fork bear right again, and the trail will lead you to a point overlooking the estuary at the mouth of the Colquitz River. Estuaries, formed where fresh water meets the sea, are shallow and rich in organic matter that has been washed downstream in sediment, which settles to form mud flats. These flats, tidal and constantly replenished, make estuaries the most fertile and productive of any ecosystem. They support many types of invertebrates, insects and larval fish, all of which are an important source of food for waterfowl, small mammals and predatory fish.

You are likely to see ducks feeding at the river mouth. These will be mostly dabblers like mallards, teal and perhaps shovellers, birds that pump the soupy water through the sieves of their spatula bills to trap edible organisms. The deeper channels are frequented by fish-eaters like buffleheads and mergansers.

Returning to the main bark-mulch path, the trail wanders through a coniferous forest, composed primarily of Douglas-firs. However, grand firs (also known as balsam firs) grow here too. Try telling the two apart by examining the leaves or needles. The Douglas-fir has flat, yellowish-green needles about 2.5 cm (1 inch) long and with pointed tips, whereas the grand fir has flat, dark-green, two-ranked needles that are slightly longer. The cone shape and bark colour and texture are other distinguishing factors, but their leaf and needle characteristics are the most reliable indicators. The undergrowth in this coniferous forest is mostly shade-loving plants such as salal, Oregon grape and sword ferns. In the spring, look for the white three-petalled flowers of the western trillium and the delicate blooms of white fawn lilies, which grow abundantly all through this forest.

About 100 m (330 feet) from the point overlooking the estuary, the main path intersects an inside trail. Then it passes over the Colquitz River by a bridge, known as Heron Bridge, and leads to another entrance to the park. If you walk onto the bridge, you may see great blue herons stalking the creek below. This was once a favourite area for the herons, but with the encroachment of human settlement their numbers have dwindled, as

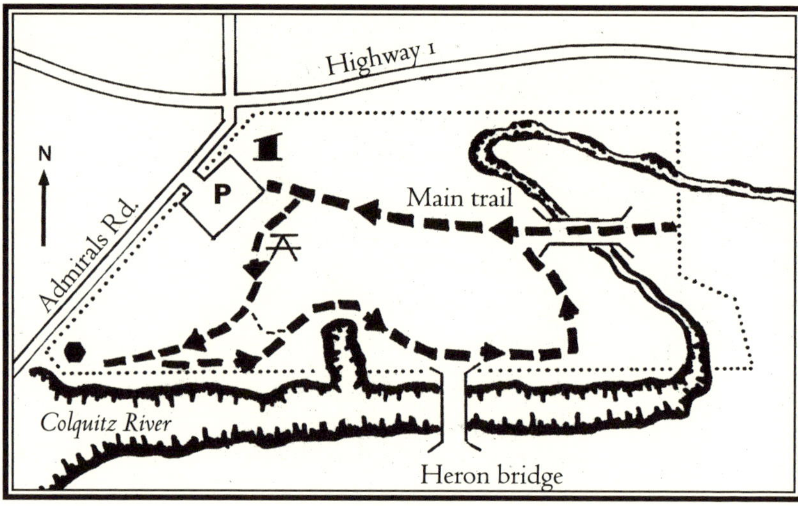

they have elsewhere. Although the park is protected the surrounding lands have been developed, and where once flocks of up to one hundred herons came to breed, one is lucky to see a few feeding. From the bridge the trail passes through a dense stand of conifers with very little undergrowth. This was the site of the recently abandoned heron rookery. If you look up about 25 m (80 feet) you may see the remnants of an old nest.

About 300 m (1000 feet) past Heron Bridge, the trail leads to a second bridge and then to the paved trail. Cross this bridge and enter a mixed wood of Garry oak, Douglas-fir, and alder with a lush undergrowth of snowberry, blackberry, little buttercup (or small-flowered buttercup) and larged-leaved aven. As you round the bend, this dank, cool forest abruptly gives way to open meadow. "Edges" like this, where different habitats meet, hold the greatest diversity of bird species, butterflies and other small creatures. Towhees, song sparrows and golden-crowned sparrows live in the tangled undergrowth most of the year and are joined in spring by orange-crowned warblers and swallowtail butterflies. Here you will once again see a meadowland in transition; the grassy areas are quickly being filled with wild rose, hawthorn and Scotch broom. Where farming has taken place in the past, hawthorns often mark old fence lines and property boundaries, just as lilacs and overgrown windbreaks indicate the site of an old farmhouse.

Since Cuthbert Holmes Park was once agricultural land, in this meadow you will find neglected apple, plum and crabapple trees from some past orchard. In May the meadow is bordered with blue-flowering camas and a scattering of the magenta-flowered common salsify. By June the flowers of the salsify are over, and you should look for their stunning seed heads, dandelion-like in shape but larger and darker. On a sunny day each seed parachute seems to be a diamond umbrella reflecting the light. Mixed with the wildflowers are numerous types of native grasses, and here you may see a savannah sparrow clinging to a grass stalk, feasting on the seeds. It is only one of the small bird species that rely heavily on plants of the edge and open land. House finches and goldfinches, in particular, flock in late summer to the blowing dandelions and the untidy patches of Canada thistle that flourish among the tangled blackberry and faded grasses.

Continue through another 500 m (1650 feet) of meadowland, and the paved path ends. This is the third entrance to the park and leads to the Pearkes Recreation Centre on Dysart Road. To return, retrace your steps, taking either the paved path back to the Admirals Road parking lot or the bark-mulch trail, which leads back via Heron Bridge. Several other side trails all lead back to Admirals Road.

HOW TO GET THERE: Cuthbert Holmes Park is located off Admirals Road. Take Highway 1 to Admirals Road. Turn south; the park entrance will be to your left soon after the turn from the highway.

8

Knockan Hill Park

SAANICH

HIGHLIGHTS: Wildflowers, rocky outcrops, vistas

WALKING LEVEL: Easy

SEASON: Spring

ATTIRE: Rainwear during winter

DOG WALKING: Allowed

ROUND TRIP: 1 km (½ mile)

THE LAST FEW YEARS have witnessed a dramatic loss of the Garry oak woodlands so characteristic of the Victoria region. In Canada, Garry oaks are restricted primarily to the southeast coast of Vancouver Island and the southern Gulf Islands. Since more than one thousand species of plants and animals and one-fifth of the rarest plants in British Columbia are found in association with Garry oaks, the reduction of this unique habitat is a serious loss. Urban development is the chief cause. It has had a devastating effect, particularly because Greater Victoria now sprawls across what was once the largest continuous occurrence of Garry oak woodlands anywhere.

Surprisingly, fire suppression has also played a destructive role by eliminating a natural check on the spread of conifers, allowing them to invade areas once dominated by Garry oaks. Exotic species such as Scotch broom and orchard grass have replaced many native species and altered the makeup of the Garry oak ecosystem. Fortunately, in the vicinity of Victoria several parks retain fine examples of Garry oak habitat. The walk described in this chapter is in such a park.

Knockan Hill is nestled in the neighbourhood of Strawberry Vale. This small park was formerly the property of two English school teachers who settled in Stranton Lodge on Burnside Road West. The lodge

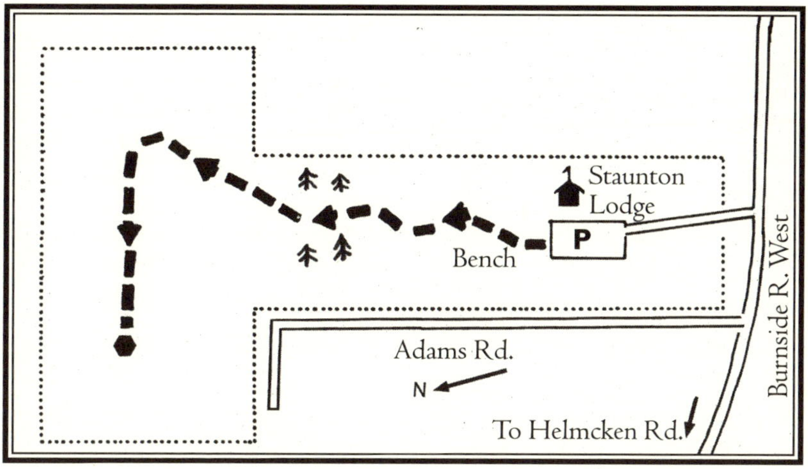

still stands, and its gardens are being rejuvenated under the joint auspices of the Friends of Knockan Hill Society and the Saanich Historical Society. Although there are several entrances to the park, take the one from Burnside Road West. Keep a lookout for the park sign and go up the driveway leading to Stranton Lodge. Although the driveway appears to belong to a private residence, do not be misled; once at the top, you will come to a small parking lot and an information board. The gravel and bark-mulch trail leads away from the information board and travels through a mixed forest of Douglas-fir and bigleaf maples. The wide trail is well maintained, and although the route is an uphill climb the grade is gentle and can be enjoyed by those with limited mobility.

Not far into the walk you will come to a wooden bridge spanning a depression, where rainwater collects during autumn and winter. A short distance beyond is a bench set among sword ferns, bracken, snowberry and ivy. This last is a non-native plant, probably English ivy, which was brought to North America by the early settlers. It is common everywhere, and you will notice that where there is a profusion of ivy, native plants are few. Most are choked out by this vigorous climber.

As you continue up the trail, notice a slight change in the surroundings. Rocky outcroppings begin to appear, as do arbutus trees and Garry oaks. These two tree species, although common in and near Victoria, are found nowhere else in Canada. Douglas-firs and grand firs still grace the forest, but short, stunted arbutus and Garry oaks become more numerous as you climb. About 200 m (660 feet) from the bench, the trail divides. Stay on the main branch, because the secondary one leads to one of many entrances that connect the park with the surrounding residential neighbourhoods. Several more secondary trails lead to park entrances and should be ignored.

As you continue, watch for an enormous rock face to the left of the trail. It is beautifully decorated with stonecrop, giving it a blush of yellow in the spring and summer when the flowers appear. Knockan is the Salish word for "rocks on a hill," an apt description of what meets the eye when you reach the summit. Here the terrain levels out and scrub Garry oaks stand among patches of bare rock. In spring a profusion of wildflowers grow beneath the trees. Among them are the easily missed white fawn lilies and the delicate pink satin flower, one of the earliest to bloom. Much easier to spot is the camas, whose robust spikes of vibrant-blue blossoms stand out against the grass. Look also for the magenta shootingstar, whose petals are drawn sharply back from its pointed stamens and style. At the base of each flower is a yellow band where bumblebees make upside-down landings, inadvertently shaking pollen from the flower's anthers onto their wings and bodies.

The views to the east overlooking Saanich from the top of Knockan Hill are breathtaking. From the other, west-facing side, the views are equally fine, embracing Observatory Hill and the surrounding countryside. The flat rocks at the top of the hill make good picnic sites from which to appreciate the views. To complete the walk, retrace your steps down to the parking lot.

HOW TO GET THERE: From Highway 1, take Helmcken Road north to Burnside Road West and turn right onto Burnside. The park entrance is about 3 blocks down the street and on the left. Note: The entrance is not well marked, and the drive to the parking lot is easily missed.

Entrance to Knockan Hill Park

9

Quick's Bottom Park

SAANICH

HIGHLIGHTS: Birdwatching, marsh plants, wildflowers

WALKING LEVEL: Easy

SEASON: All year

ATTIRE: Waterproof shoes in rainy season

DOG WALKING: Not allowed

ROUND TRIP: 1.5 km (1 mile)

QUICK'S BOTTOM, A 20-HA (50-acre) wetland park, offers a gentle walk through meadows and marshland. Once cultivated as farmland, this area became a municipal park in 1977 and will particularly appeal to people who enjoy birdwatching but do not care for an arduous trek over difficult terrain. There are three entrances to Quick's Bottom, two on Markham Street and one leading from Wilkinson Road.

The walk described in this chapter begins at the Wilkinson Road entrance, where a bark-mulch path gently slopes downward. Beneath the branches of Douglas-firs and bigleaf maples the way is lined with shrubbery, mostly a mixed growth of snowberries, ferns, blackberries and ivy. Approximately 40 m (130 feet) along the path look for stands of bitter cherry, whose clusters of small white flowers turn into red pea-sized "cherries" in late summer. In early summer the ground beneath these trees is covered by the blooms of the little small-flowered buttercup, a 20–90-cm (8–36-inch)-tall perennial that produces very small, five-petal, yellow flowers, several to a stem.

Following the path, you will come to a wooden bridge passing over a stream, now stagnant and covered with brilliant-green algae. Look to the right and you will see the Pacific ninebark growing along the stream bed. In late spring and early summer this tangled shrub, with its shiny, dark-

Sora rail

green leaves, is covered with small clusters of white flowers with pink stamens. The branches of the ninebark turn brown as they age, with distinctive shredding bark, and by midsummer its flowers are being replaced by reddish clumps of seed husks. Across the bridge, the trail climbs upward, between banks of frothy ocean spray, sweet-scented wild rose, fir and cedar.

This mixture soon gives way to hedgerows of common and black hawthorns. Their flowering in the late spring makes this part of the walk a mass of pink and white blossoms. Rounding the bend of the trail, you will briefly see the low-lying wetland, or "bottom," before the trail continues between more hawthorn and Nootka rose. Most of the wild rose in this park is of this species, which may grow 3 m (10 feet) high, with sweet-scented, white to deep-rose flowers up to 8 cm (3 inches) across

Late summer flowers at Quick's Bottom

from May to July. Its brilliant scarlet hips, brighter than the hawthorn berries, hang like Christmas tree ornaments all through the winter and, in their way, are as beautiful as the blooms of early summer.

About 250 m (825 feet) from the bridge, the bark-mulch trail turns into a gravel path and the hawthorn hedges give way to open vistas of the marsh. The tall, grey-green grass that grows profusely here is reed canary grass, *Phalaris arundinacea,* a long-lived perennial 2 m (6½ feet) tall and able to withstand extreme wet and dry conditions. This alien grass is an import from Europe and is used as forage all over North America. When the land in and around Quick's Bottom was farmed, the reed canary grass was kept in check by cultivation or cattle. The marsh flooded in winter, and when the weather was cold enough, its frozen surface was a great attraction to the skaters of Victoria. When it became a park farming was discontinued, and the reed canary grass, cattails and other vegetation quickly invaded the marshy flats. These flats are turning into grassland and, if left to themselves, will eventually become forest.

Looking across the diminishing marsh, you will see a copse of fir trees in the distance, beyond a stand of black cottonwood. Nearby are young hawthorn and cottonwood trees, willows, bitter cherry and wild rose and, finally, at the marsh's rim, the reed canary grass and cattails, their roots in water. These groupings mark stages in a natural plant succession that occurs as the chemical and physical characteristics of the soil gradually change as a result of the decomposition of plants and other organic matter. At Quick's Bottom this is regretted not only by skaters, who are losing their rustic arena, but also by birders, who found the marsh rich in unusual species.

Although reed canary grass is the dominant species in Quick's Bottom, many other plants also grow here. If you bring a pocket plant-identification guide, try to identify marsh cinquefoil, narrow-leaved bur-reed, and common mare's-tail, all of which form the mats of vegetation used by pied-billed grebes as foundations of their floating nest platforms. Look for the bright yellow flowers of the low-growing silver weed or the taller American brooklime, whose delicate flowers range in shades from violet blue to pale lilac. This marsh formerly provided a habitat for native amphibians such as the Pacific tree frog and the Pacific coast newt, but it has recently become home to thoughtlessly introduced bullfrogs, which have virtually eliminated the native species.

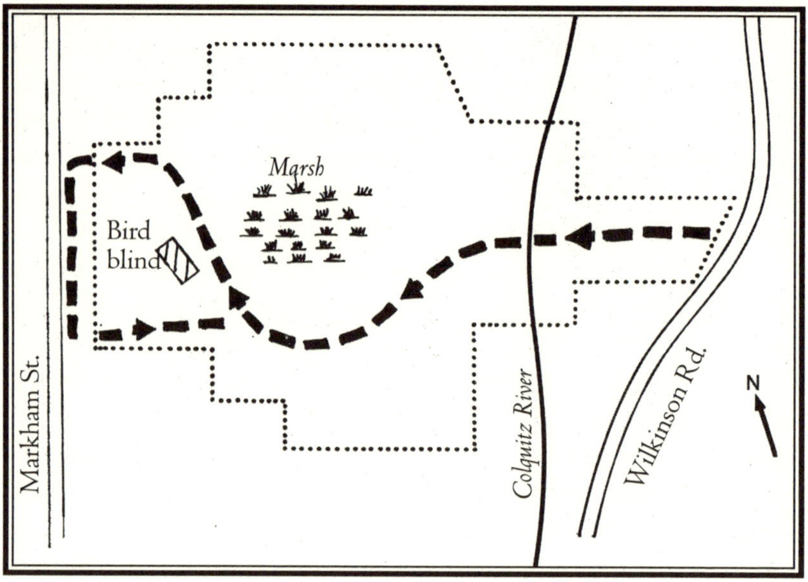

As the trail continues, the gravel path again becomes a bark-mulch trail. About 75 m (250 feet) beyond the change, a fork appears in the trail. The straight branch is a 100-m (330-foot) route to the second entrance to the park from Markham Street and away from the low-lying area. Both sides of this path feature plants that prefer drier ground: pink and white clover, ox-eye daisies, vetch, thistle and many types of native grasses. If you take the right fork in the trail, you can either stop to rest on a conveniently placed bench or cross a second wooden bridge and continue along the tree-lined trail for 50 m (165 feet), where you will emerge to a full view of the marsh. On the left-hand side is a broad bed of cattails, the scene of much singing and displaying by red-winged blackbirds in the breeding season. It is also a likely place to see a yellowthroat, the small, black-masked warbler with the emphatic song. In early summer, look for the golden-eyed grass that makes brilliant splashes of yellow when in bloom.

At the other side of the trail is a bird blind, from which you can observe some of the many kinds of birds that inhabit the marsh. At any time of the year there is something to see; green-winged teals are almost always dabbling in the shallows, and if you are lucky you may see the rare, brick-red cinnamon teal, which occasionally breeds here. A variety of other ducks use the marsh, particularly in winter. They include surface feeders like widgeons, shovellers and even wood ducks, as well as divers like the smartly painted ring-necked ducks. By patient waiting, or sometimes just by chance, you may spot a sora rail as it feeds among the water plants. This elusive bird is not uncommon, but it is extremely shy, preferring the shelter of the grasses and sedges to life in the open. Peregrine falcons are frequently seen here, as are bald eagles.

The trail continues past another wooden bench, surrounded in April and May by common camas and other wildflowers in their season. Although you cannot see the marsh when sitting on the bench, there is still much to engage your attention. Warm weather brings out the early butterflies—first the little "blues" and tortoiseshells, and later, showy tiger swallowtails, whose stripy green caterpillars feed on cottonwood leaves and willow. In early spring you may see a chocolate-coloured butterfly, the mourning cloak, sunning its cream-bordered wings on the path. It may have hatched late in the previous summer and overwintered here as an adult. From the bench, look to your left and you will see two large Garry oaks, an indication that this side of the park is much drier than the other.

From here the path ascends gently, now bordered by Garry oak, snowberry and bitter cherry. The track levels and then descends to a left-hand turn and the end of the marsh. This last section of the trail marks the border of the park and is lined with a fence. Continuing along the trail you will come to the third entrance to the park, again on Markham Street. From this point you can either retrace your steps or walk about 350 m (1150 feet) along Markham Street to the other entrance, where you can again pick up the trail (as shown on the map).

HOW TO GET THERE: Quick's Bottom is located off Wilkinson Road. From Highway 17, take Royal Oak Drive west. After crossing West Saanich Road, Royal Oak becomes Wilkinson Road. Follow Wilkinson for about 0.5 km (⅓ mile) and watch for the "Quick's Bottom Park" sign.

10

Beaver Lake

ELK/BEAVER LAKE REGIONAL PARK SAANICH

HIGHLIGHTS: Birdwatching, lake views, large conifers

WALKING LEVEL: Easy; wheelchair accessible

SEASON: All year

ATTIRE: Rainwear in wet months

DOG WALKING: Dogs must be under control at all times; not allowed on beaches June 1–September 15

ROUND TRIP: 1 km (½ mile)

ONE OF THE MOST popular and intensively used parks in the Victoria area is Elk/Beaver Lake Regional Park. Covering 411 ha (1025 acres), it encompasses two bodies of water, Elk and Beaver Lakes, which were once separate but since the damming of Colquitz Creek have been joined by a narrow passage. The lakes became a source of water for Greater Victoria in 1872 and continued to supply certain areas until 1977. The walk described in this chapter follows one of many trails in the park and is recommended for wheelchair users and people who prefer a gentle route. Since the course travels a figure-eight, those who wish a short amble can cut across and circle back halfway.

From the Beaver Lake parking lot at the North Beach, go past the changing rooms and concession stand and look for a gravel path. This wide path is marked with the signpost, "No horses or bikes." The first half of the trail runs beside Beaver Lake and through a mixed coniferous and deciduous forest of large Douglas-firs, grand firs, cottonwoods, bigleaf maples and western red cedars. The large conifers stand right next to the trail, allowing you to get a close look at the various species and to

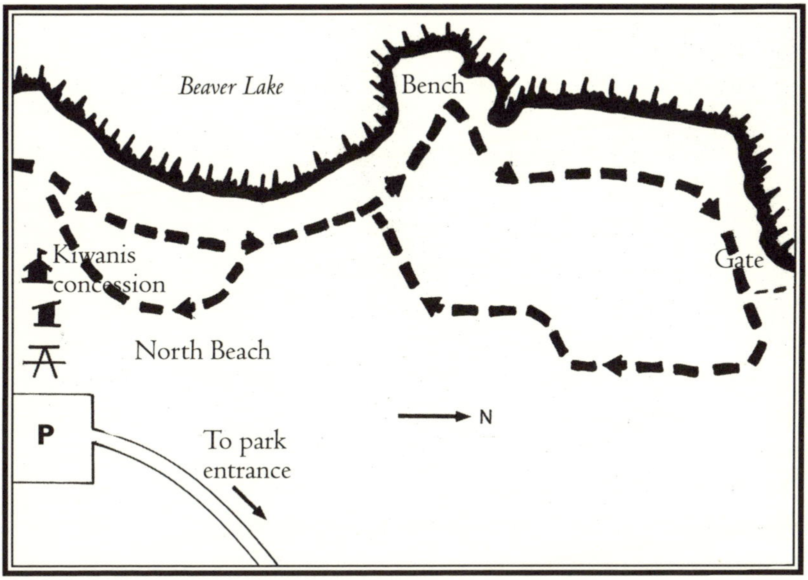

note each one's identifying peculiarities. For example, if you spot a resin blister on the trunk, the tree is a grand fir, not a Douglas-fir. Pop the blister and smell the "balsam" odour of the resin, which is an effective ointment for mosquito bites. The blistering of the bark is a characteristic of all true firs in British Columbia. Despite its name, the Douglas-fir is not a true fir but a member of the *Pseudotsuga* family, which do not have blistering bark.

About 350 m (1150 feet) from the start of the walk you will come to a small, sandy beach often used by picnickers and swimmers on hot summer afternoons. Look along the beach to the right and you will see a large rototiller; this is used to remove the roots of Eurasian water milfoil, a notoriously invasive, accidentally introduced aquatic plant that smothers and destroys native communities of aquatic plants wherever it appears. It is easily carried from one lake to another on the hulls of recreational boats and is very difficult to control once it is established. Eurasian milfoil is not the only exotic arrival on the lake, though it is the worst.

Almost as alien as the milfoil, but much less pernicious, are the Canada geese you will see out on the water. Two or three races of this magnificent waterfowl migrate along the Pacific flyway, but the Elk Lake birds, descendants of an introduced flock, are big, pale, transplanted Easterners. They have thrived and multiplied to become year-round residents and, still on the increase, may be seen grazing on the fields of the Saanich Peninsula.

Continuing on the path, about 25 m (80 feet) along, you will come to another sign that bans biking and horses. Here, under the canopy of large trees, the trail is damper. Moss clings to the bark of the bigleaf maples, and among the ferns in summer there are plenty of Cooley's stinging nettles, where reddish-purple, deep-throated flowers attract hummingbirds. On the lake side of the path you will catch intermittent glimpses of the water between the thickets of willow and hardhack, and about 100 m (330 feet) along there is a cement sluice to one side of the path.

This walk is particularly good for birdwatchers. In the quiet of the heavily forested trail you may hear the eerie, slightly discordant whistle of the varied thrush, the deep notes of a raven or the rasping call of a jay. Look for signs of nesting barred owls. These dark-eyed, round-headed birds use the cavities of tree stumps and sometimes nest right beside the trail. Great horned owls, yellow-eyed and "eared," also can be found in these woods, and like barred owls they may sometimes be seen in daytime. Pileated woodpeckers drum and cackle while, in the canopy, chickadees and kinglets reveal their presence with thin call notes.

Not far along is a wooden bench from which you have a beautiful view across Beaver Lake. In the foreground, rushes and willows grow at the water's edge while stands of conifers make blocks of a darker colour on the far side. After continuing about 325 m (1000 feet) down the trail, you will come to another signpost. You can cut short your walk here, making a loop back to the parking lot by bearing right and following the arrow pointing to North Beach. If you wish to continue, take the lakeside path, bearing left, and avoid the middle trail, which goes inland and is marked as a bridle path.

On this section the ground becomes drier, and you will notice the change in the vegetation. The trail, which follows the lake about 50 m (165 feet) inland, is bordered by cottonwood, Nootka rose and tall willows that obscure the view of the water. On the land side of the trail, honeysuckle winds around ocean spray and there are frequent stands of young alder. Not far down the trail, the path returns to the lakeshore, where a

Tree stump in Beaver Lake

bench has been provided for those in need of a rest. It overlooks a small, still bay, where yellow-flowering pond lilies cover the surface of the water and kingfishers come to hunt. Here lives another alien resident of these waters—the bullfrog, introduced to Beaver Lake several years ago and thriving. In a way unhappily characteristic of plants and animals introduced into places where they have no business, it eats anything that fits in its mouth, including small birds and native amphibians.

About 500 m (1600 feet) down the trail, you will come to a wooden turnstile. Do not go through the turnstile unless you wish to walk around Elk Lake and the far side of Beaver Lake, a distance of about 10 km (6 miles). Keep on the gravel path and bear right. A sign pointing to Beaver Lake will take you on an inland route back to the parking lot. As the path winds away from the lake, the vegetation changes. No longer do you see large stands of conifers. Instead, thickets of Nootka rose, red-osier dogwood and cottonwoods grow in open meadows. Black-headed grosbeaks have been seen here, and in fact this is prime grosbeak habitat. In early April look for the bulky, black-and-burnt-orange males singing their hurried, robin-like song from some elevated perch.

After another signpost directing walkers to Beaver Lake, the open meadows give way to forest, and once again the path passes through a darker, shadier area, where large Douglas-firs, grand firs and cedars flourish. Look for a stand of Douglas-fir that has been worked by hairy woodpeckers. The excavations they have made in order to feed are mostly near the base of the trees and do not extend far up the trunks.

About 500 m (1600 feet) from the last signpost, the trail returns to the point where the paths intersected halfway through the walk. If you are in a wheelchair or wish a gentler return route, take the lakeside trail, the same path you took in the first section of the walk. If not, keep to your left and travel away from the lake, going uphill through an open area with a profusion of ocean spray. This is a slow but steady incline to the top of the hill, from which the path winds down through an old forest of western red cedars, Douglas-firs and bigleaf maples that have grown to a considerable size.

Look for the "1 km" marker, which has been erected for the many runners who use this trail. When you reach the bottom of the descent, a boardwalk over a small stream will lead to the last few hundred metres of trail, which returns to the North Beach and parking lot.

HOW TO GET THERE: Beaver Lake is located off the Pat Bay Highway. From Highway 17, turn west onto Elk Lake Drive. Take Elk Lake Drive, which curves southward, to Beaver Lake Road. Turn right onto Beaver Lake Road, and right again to the North Beach parking lot.

11

Bear Hill Regional Park

SAANICH

HIGHLIGHTS: Wildflowers, Garry oaks, rock striations, raptor watching

WALKING LEVEL: Difficult

SEASON: Spring and summer

ATTIRE: Sturdy walking shoes

DOG WALKING: Excellent

ROUND TRIP: 2 km (1¼ miles)

ON THE SAANICH PENINSULA, in the heart of Victoria's farmland, lies Bear Hill, a 50-ha (125-acre) park with outstanding views of Sidney, the San Juan Islands and the waters between. Although this is a difficult walk, the ascent to the summit is only about 1 km (⅔ mile) long and is well worth the effort.

At the park's main entrance on Bear Hill Road there is a small parking lot, just before the trailhead, with enough room for about six cars. The beginning of the path is steep and has a loose-gravel surface, so walk carefully, especially in wet weather. The trail takes you through some typical Garry oak–arbutus woodland with an admixture of Douglas-firs, bigleaf maples and cedars. The shrubbery includes ferns, blackberry, salal and snowberry.

If you are here in spring, this part of the walk offers one of the most stunning displays of wildflowers imaginable. But keep your eyes open: some of the more delicate plants here are unobtrusive and easily over-

Rock patch on Bear Hill

looked. Look for the wildflowers that are always associated with Garry oaks, such as satin flowers in March, camas and fawn lilies a few weeks later. In summer you can't miss the flowering cascades of the aptly named ocean spray or the native grasses that form a carpet of yellows, pinks and greens. In late summer and fall, the branches of the Garry oaks drip with grey-green lichens and their trunks are clothed in velvety mosses. About 100 m (330 feet) from the start of the trail, look toward the rock crevice on your left, where in early summer the nodding onion blooms. Its umbrellas of pale pink-to-purple flowers hang in clusters on single stalks, and, unless you notice their strong onion smell, they can be missed. More obvious are the many huckleberry bushes along the trail. Black bears love their small, vivid red berries, and seeing huckleberries here is a reminder that not so many years ago bears really did roam the hill.

The trail flattens temporarily about 50 m (165 feet) along and passes through a stand of Douglas-firs that give walkers some welcome shade on a hot day. If you are interested in birds, early summer is perhaps the best time for viewing, but even in winter keep an eye out for nests. Those of songbirds are often small masterpieces of building and are difficult to discover in summer, when the trees are in leaf. I once came across a bulky structure of sticks about 10 m (30 feet) up in one of the Douglas-firs. Although large, it was not big enough or high enough to be the nest of an eagle, but a Cooper's hawk feather on the ground below gave a clue to the nester's identity.

Another surprising find in this wooded area is the Indian pipe, or ghost-plant, which pokes its head through the soil in early summer. A member of a family known as saprophytes, it has no chlorophyll and derives its nourishment not by photosynthesis but from decaying vegetable matter. Look for clusters of this curious plant near decaying wood or fallen trees. The pallid stems are an unusual sight and look like old-fashioned clay pipes stuck into the ground. As they age, the waxy, fleshy stems turn black, and the single nodding flower, the "bowl" of the pipe, that caps each one becomes erect as the seeds develop. Indian pipe is not the only saprophyte on Bear Hill; there are also choral bells and pinedrops. It is, however, the only one growing in extensive clusters.

Also growing in this section of the walk is a purple flowering perennial called self-heal, or heal-all. This non-native species can be identified by its bonnet-like flowers on short stalks with smooth leaves. As its name

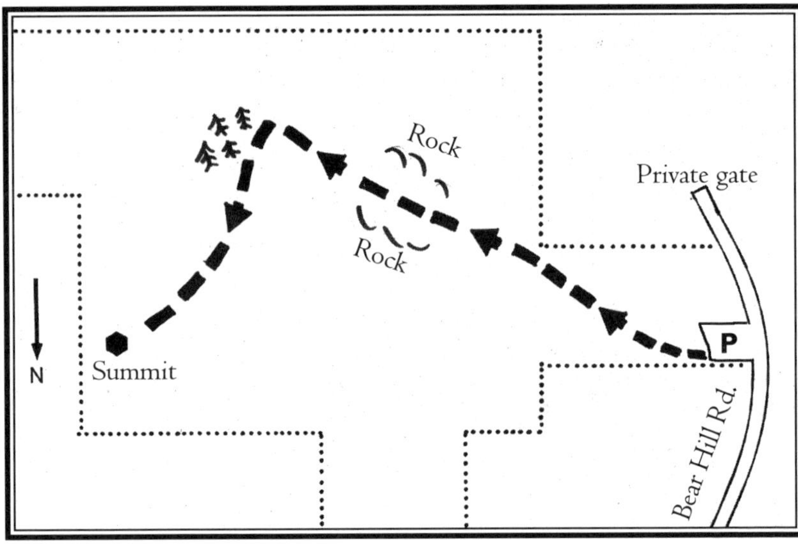

suggests, this member of the mint family reputedly has medicinal properties. Brewed as weak tea, it was taken as a tonic for heart trouble, and skin irritations were treated with a dressing of its leaves.

The path now winds through a kind of impoverished Garry oak–arbutus woodland that often appears where conditions are dry and comparatively harsh. Here the Garry oaks are low and scrubby, a far cry from the giants found in more sheltered oak meadows like Uplands Park. Growing on this part of Bear Hill, they must make the best of the shallow soil and extreme dryness.

As you climb Bear Hill to the summit you will notice bare rock surfaces beside the path, a testament to the hardness of the bedrock here. Bear Hill is an example of a monadnock, a column of rock hard enough to have resisted erosion during the last glaciation. As the glacier advanced, the great mass of ice scraped away the softer and looser surface sediment but left the harder rock exposed. Evidence of the powerful force of the moving ice is apparent in the striations or furrows that still mark the hard surfaces of Bear Hill's rock. Other monadnocks in the Victoria region include Mount Tolmie, Mount Douglas and Mount Newton.

Looking west from this elevation, you can see the berry fields and sheep pastures of Oldfield Road. Patches of dark woodland punctuate the pastoral greens and yellows of the cultivated land. You may have the unusual experience of being above the red-tailed hawks that soar over the open land and raise their young on the wooded heights. From April until September the red-tails share their air space, though not their taste for small rodents, with great, black-winged turkey vultures. The vultures are beautiful in the air, and only when they are at rest do they seem as unsavoury as their reputation. Comparative newcomers to Victoria, they now nest in the area, raising their single chicks in caves and crevices on rocky bluffs like those of Bear Hill. The young birds of late summer can be identified by their black heads (adults have pink heads), and both can be distinguished from young, all-dark eagles by the slight upward angle of their wings in flight.

As you wind around the last section of the trail, you will see a sign that reads "Summit." The path takes you to the other side of the hill and through a level, moister wooded area of Douglas-fir, arbutus, salal and Oregon grape. If you look closely, you may find more Indian pipe. Garry oaks are rare here because they are even less tolerant than arbutus of the damp conditions. After walking about 75 m (250 feet) you will come to another "Summit" sign. Bear right, ignoring the many other trails that lead to other parts of the hill. The summit trail travels a short distance to the top where, having completed the 220-m (725-foot) climb, you have a spectacular view of the Saanich Peninsula and the San Juan Islands to the east and south and of Sidney to the north. The summit's flat rock surfaces make this spot perfect for lazy picnics on hot summer days or for just a rest before the return trip.

HOW TO GET THERE: Bear Hill Park is located at Bear Hill Road. From Highway 17, turn west onto Sayward Road. Then turn left onto Hamsterly Road and right onto Brookleigh Road. Continue along Brookleigh to Oldfield Road. Turn right onto Oldfield and then right again onto Bear Hill Road. Follow Bear Hill Road to the parking lot.

12

Island View Beach Regional Park

CENTRAL SAANICH

HIGHLIGHTS: Birdwatching, beachcombing, sand dunes, beach flowers, picnic area

WALKING LEVEL: Easy

SEASON: Winter

ATTIRE: Rainwear and waterproof shoes in winter

DOG WALKING: Dogs must be on a leash or under control at all times and are not allowed in the picnic area or on beaches June 1–September 15

ROUND TRIP: 2 km (1¼ miles)

FOR WALKERS INTERESTED IN shorebirds and sand dunes, Island View Beach is the best and closest beach walk in the Victoria region. The park was created in 1966; originally consisting of one 30-ha (75-acre) area, it was enlarged by adding a second, 10.5-ha (25-acre) area at its south end in 1992. The park can be reached via the beach or from Homathko Drive. There are parking lots both at the eastern end of Island View Road and at the north end of Homathko Drive, where you will also find wheelchair-accessible washroom facilities.

It is well worth the effort to leave your car in the first parking lot and walk the 200 m (650 feet) north along the beach to the park entrance. This beach is constantly changing because of exposure to storms and ocean currents. At this south end of the park, the waves crash head-on and surge back too powerfully to allow the depositing of fine sand. Instead, the shore consists of rock and coarse gravel, material washed from the eroding cliffs of James Island, which lies directly across the water, and from Cowichan Head lying to the south. Beach pea, silverweed and yellow sand verbena bravely cling to pockets of sandy soil, surviving the harsh conditions by spreading outward and growing low to the ground. The fleshy, succulent leaves of the yellow sand verbena store moisture from dew and fog, and by shedding old leaves the plant excretes excess sea salt.

In winter, the shore is buffeted by strong southeasterly winds and the intertidal life is not rich. The many species common in soft sand or on rocky shores are not found here. Nevertheless, whelks and acorn barnacles cling to the lee sides of the larger rocks, and on some of the boulders white circular spots mark the sites of old barnacle colonies. Turn over a rock or log and you may find a purple shore crab or a gunnel living in the water-filled depression. Put the rock or log back in its original position so that these creatures can survive until the next high tide.

A little farther on the beach starts to curve, and you will become conscious of a change underfoot as rocks are replaced by sand. Here the waves strike the beach at an oblique angle, and their resulting loss of force permits the formation of a sandier, less hostile shore. At low tide look for small holes in the wet sand, indicating clams below the surface. Through these holes the clams thrust their rubbery, snorkel-like siphons at high tide and lie safely buried in the sand while feeding on tiny organisms in the water. At low tide a clam remains relaxed in its hole, but it will pull in its siphon and slam shut its shell if disturbed, expelling the water in its body cavity. This is the cause of the little jets of water you will sometimes see when walking the wet sands at low tide.

At certain times of the year Island View Beach is especially good for birds. In late July, flocks of shorebirds—the various, small, difficult-to-tell-apart sandpipers or "peeps"—begin their long southward migration from their tundra breeding grounds by following the Pacific flyway, an ancient and invariable route along the edge of the continent. This flyway is used by many other species, including birds of prey, and you may see a peregrine falcon beating along the coastline or glimpse the swift form of a black merlin as it harries a flock of dunlins. Loons of all three common species, as well as red-necked, western and horned grebes, gather offshore, sometimes in the thousands, to feed on herring. Seeing them well requires a powerful spotting scope, but a pair of binoculars is all that is necessary for the scoters, harlequins, goldeneyes and other ducks that frequent the waters closer to shore. These are mussel-eating ducks, with stout, boot-shaped bills that are strong enough to wrench shellfish from their moorings. The fish-eating ducks like mergansers are here, too, as are murres, guillemots, auklets and, of course, gulls.

Approximately 200 m (650 feet) along the beach, at the far end of the RV park, look for a sign marked "Paws Here Rover." This sign marks the beach entrance to the northern section of Island View Beach Park. From here you can climb up to the gravel track that runs the length of the berm, a raised embankment. As you walk along it, notice the difference in the growing habits of the plants on either side of the trail. On the shore side the plants are shorter and have fleshier leaves than those on the sheltered side, where the same species grow much taller. This adaptation to prevailing conditions is especially visible in silver burweed and lupins. Farther along the walk, a scattering of logs lies just below the berm. Sand has been trapped in the shelter of these logs, allowing vegetation to flourish. Beyond the logs the wind has formed fragile sand dunes, their unstable contours dictated by storms. The fluid character of the shoreline is exemplified by these shifting dunes, which may be present one year and gone the next.

Approximately halfway along the trail, it is intersected by another path leading to public toilets. As you continue along the berm trail, look away from the ocean and you will see a low-lying, flat area, which in spring and summer is clothed in silverweed and common velvet grass, forming a carpet of yellow, chartreuse green and silvery pink. These moisture-loving plants mark a change in the terrain. In winter it is often under water, flooded by the runoff from nearby cliffs. An area like this is known as a "slack" or "winter-loch," and is typically found beyond a sand-dune beach. It was on such a slack, at St. Andrews, Scotland, that golf was invented in 1411, the flat land there providing the fairways and the dunes the rough. Above this and other open stretches of the park, red-tailed hawks often soar as they search the land below for small rodents. Closer to the ground, look for the longer-winged, buoyant outline of a harrier as it quarters the grass. It, too, is after small prey, and every now and then you will see it drop suddenly on some hapless vole or deer mouse.

The trail continues a little farther along the berm and then descends a slope to a sandy parallel path. The slope is narrow, but at the bottom the

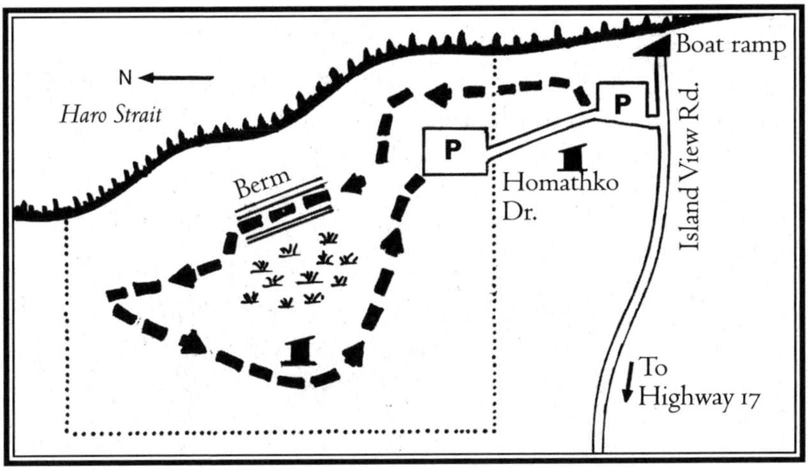

trail widens and is well marked with driftwood. Plants along this path are denser, and their variety is greater than before; shrubs are mixed in with perennials, grasses, sedges and rushes. Try to distinguish grasses from rushes, and sedges and rushes from each other. The old adage is, "Sedges have edges and rushes are round." Both have solid or pithy stems, whereas grass stems are hollow.

During summer the variety of grasses, sedges and rushes at Island View Beach Park gives a glorious display of cinnamon reds, golden yellows and silvery blues, which add much to the surroundings. These plants appear to be growing out of sand. Kick the sand, however, and you will see brown, organic matter underneath the top layer. This shows clearly the natural change in soil composition that takes place over time. Many years ago the inward side of the berm was part of the beach, but the annual decomposition of plant matter has enriched the original sand, altering its composition and allowing new plant species to take root.

This sandy trail will bring you to the border of the park, passing over a flat patch of dry land that is home to beach carrot and other drought-tolerant plants. Look for the early-blooming harvest crocus in June, with its leafless stalk and clusters of tiny, purple-pink flowers. At the park boundary, take the path to your left (the inward side) and proceed along this trail to complete a loop of the park. Pacific crabapple, Nootka rose and red elderberry growing along the way make the borders a mass of pale pink blooms in the spring, while in the level golden light of autumn

Walking the berm at Island View Beach

and winter the same hedgerows are hung with hips and great bunches of scarlet berries.

For the birder, the shrubbery and the open grassy parts of the park may produce white or golden-crowned sparrows or savannah sparrows, particularly in migration time, when these birds travel in flocks. The trail eventually passes a drainage ditch, which in spring and summer is a good place for dragonflies. These and the smaller, electric-blue damsel flies take to the wing only when the sun is shining, and a passing cloud will cause their temporary disappearance.

From here a path leads back to the beach trail, but it is only a 50-m (165-foot) walk along the inland trail to the second car park, from where you can either return to the beach or walk south on Homathko Drive back to the first car park.

HOW TO GET THERE: Island View Beach is located off Homathko Drive. Take Highway 17 to Island View Road, where there is a traffic light. Turn east onto Island View Road, travel through Martindale flats down to Homathko Drive, and park in the first parking lot.

13

John Dean Provincial Park

NORTH SAANICH

HIGHLIGHTS: Douglas-fir old-growth forest, wildflowers, vistas, fungi

WALKING LEVEL: Moderate; partially wheelchair accessible

SEASON: All year

ATTIRE: Sturdy walking shoes and rainwear in winter

DOG WALKING: Excellent

ROUND TRIP: 2.5 km (1½ miles)

IN 1921 JOHN DEAN, a long-time resident of Saanich, donated 32 ha (80 acres) of his Mount Newton property to the province for parkland. This was the first privately donated parkland in British Columbia. Further land donations over the years, from Barret Montfort, Ruth Woodward, Sydney Pickles, A. Collins and the provincial government, have increased the size of the park to 174 ha (435 acres). Since 1984, the province has been assisted by the Friends of John Dean Park association in building and maintaining the trails and preventing plant and soil degradation. The park has benefited enormously from their efforts and offers beautiful walks through one of the best examples of Douglas-fir old-growth forest anywhere on southern Vancouver Island.

Following is a description of two trails that may be walked consecutively or separately. The first walk, the West Viewpoint trail, is a 1-km (⅔-mile) climb to a lookout over Brentwood Bay and Finlayson Arm. The second is the Woodward trail, which travels through rugged country for 2 km (1¼ miles) and is one of the most beautiful trails in the park. To reach the trailhead of either walk, take the main trail from the parking lot to the Freeman King picnic area, where there are tables, washrooms and water. This, the only wheelchair-accessible path in the park, travels down a valley through a fine old-growth Douglas-fir and cedar forest, rich in vegetation such as huckleberry, Oregon grape and trailing blackberry. Although there is much debris here, scattered about from past windstorms, there is a well-groomed quality to the walk owing to the wide, sharply edged, gravel path.

From the parking lot, proceed to the picnic area continue on the gravel path. If you ignore a compact dirt trail that forks off about 75 m (250 feet) along, you will come quite soon to a lovely lily pond. It is a peaceful and contemplative place, where delicate turquoise damselflies shimmer over the surface on summer afternoons and dragonflies hawk for insect prey. The pond is home to a variety of amphibians; in spring, look for Pacific Coast newts when they congregate in the pond to spawn. Also keep an eye out for the little Pacific tree frogs, which also come here to spawn. As the days grow warmer the ardent males gather and begin calling, swelling their resonating sacs like grotesque balloons to amplify their song. The chorus of their voices can be heard at a great distance.

A short distance down the trail will bring you to another division, the left side leading up a flight of wooden stairs and the right crossing a wooden bridge. The stairs mark the start of the West Viewpoint trail, a steady climb of about 100 m (330 feet) winding through mixed forest. As you proceed along this trail you will pass through various ecosystems that become progressively drier as you climb. In this lower section, although the trees are spindly, there is a damp quality to the forest, as indicated by the richness of the mosses. However, after about 400 m (1300 feet) you are at a slightly higher elevation and will see a distinct change in the vegetation. This is marked by the appearance of arbutus trees and the ocean spray and salal that usually accompany them. Douglas-fir is still the dominant species in this woodland, but the trees are not the giants that grow at the lower elevations.

A short walk farther brings you to a branch in the trail. The left path is the Woodward trail, which is described later in this chapter. To remain on the West Viewpoint trail bear right, and later bear right again at the

Freeman King picnic area in John Dean Park

next fork. From here it is only a short distance to the viewpoint, which is marked by a sign. The climb is well worth the exertion, for the view overlooking the waters of Brentwood Bay and Finlayson Arm is spectacular. You will find yourself in a grassy clearing, a mass of pinks, yellows and blues in spring and attractive in any season. In early summer look for the orange-flowered honeysuckle, which is prolific in the park. One hot summer day when walking this trail I was rewarded by the sight of a honeysuckle vine cascading through the branches of an arbutus in this clearing. The burnt orange of the arbutus bark was the most perfect and artistic of backdrops for the torrent of orange trumpets, reminding me once again that nature is the best landscape designer of all.

Keep an eye out for the hummingbirds that journey to the Victoria area and find the nectar of the native honeysuckle particularly sweet. Although the region now has a population of Anna's hummingbirds, recent pioneers from California, the rufous hummingbird is probably the only species you will see. In honeysuckle time the tiny males, glowing like hot coals, do their incredible courtship dances, towering and diving between their sipping of nectar. The lookout is a lovely place to have a picnic, providing rocks to sit on and wonderful views to enjoy.

The lookout is the end of the West Viewpoint trail. To return to the parking lot, simply retrace your steps. If you wish to walk the Woodward trail, retrace your steps past the Surveyor's trail (the first fork on the way back) and continue along the West Viewpoint path to its juncture with the Woodward trail. The Woodward trail is not as wide or well-maintained as the West Viewpoint trail, and the route is slightly more challenging. There are, however, no major obstacles to overcome, and the beauty of this walk makes it well worth the extra effort.

Like many other trails in the park, this trail is prime habitat for mushrooms—so good, in fact, that more than one hundred species of mushrooms and other fungi have been recorded here. In late summer look for the rose-pink capped rosy gomphidius sprouting up under conifers such as Douglas-fir. Its appearance signals the beginning of mushroom season and is showy enough to attract the attention of the most casual passer-by. With a cap up to 10 cm (4 inches) across and a white stalk of 7.5 cm (3 inches) or more, this mushroom resembles a giant nail driven into the earth. Another exciting find, not so big or early seen, is the golden trumpet, a tiny yellow-orange mushroom that appears in clusters on rotting logs and stumps. Velvet foot can also be found in clusters on decaying logs, its reddish-yellow or reddish-brown 2.5–5-cm (1–2-inch) cap having a central bump and a sticky appearance. Also known as the winter mushroom, it will fruit even in the winter months, if the weather is particularly temperate.

From the trailhead, travel down to a stagnant pond surrounded by cedars. This is the top end of Emerald Pool, but might just as well be named "Mosquito Haven" because the inert water provides perfect conditions for breeding mosquitoes. For those whose interest in mosquitoes extends beyond swatting, there are two major species of mosquitoes on Vancouver Island, the *Aedes* and the *Anopheles*. While the *Aedes* and all other

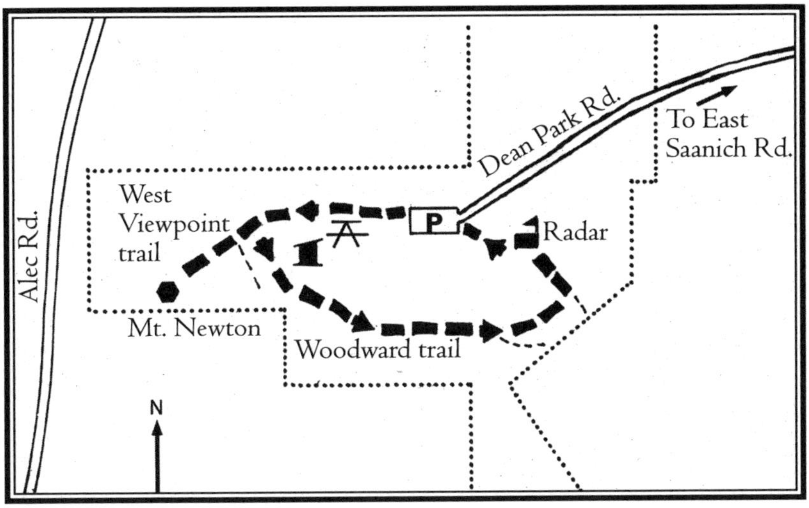

species stand straight-backed when feeding, the *Anopheles* mosquito kneels, with its body inclined and its back legs up. It is also the carrier of malaria.

The path continues to the far side of the pool and over a stone bridge. During the rainy months the ground here is wet and muddy, but the trail soon continues downhill through a drier section, where a tangle of blowdowns litters the forest floor. After about 500 m (1600 feet) you will reach the far end of Emerald Pool, from which a small stream runs. Leaving the pool behind, the trail proceeds uphill to where the conifers are smaller and more spindly because of the increased dryness.

About 350 m (1100 feet) from Emerald Pool a signpost marks the junction of the Thompson, Surveyor's and Woodward trails. For the time being, at least, the Woodward trail is the one you want. It will take you to higher ground, where Garry oaks, arbutus and Douglas-firs dot the landscape. The trail travels along a ridge where, in spring, a mass of wildflowers provides a beautiful show. Walk quietly in this area and you may spot one of the Columbian black-tailed deer that roam the park.

Once past the ridge, look for the sign marking the Lauwelnew trail. Follow this and proceed, still going uphill, as the path threads its way among rock outcroppings of exposed rock. The bare surfaces of these outcrops are softened by pockets of stonecrop and licorice ferns, while the surrounding oaks, arbutus and frothy ocean spray mitigate the rather spare dryness of the landscape.

Although it continually travels uphill the path is not difficult, and stone steps have been placed in the steeper parts. The trail continues to Pickles Bluff, where grassy knolls provide good resting places and the view of the Saanich Peninsula and James Island is outstanding. Mount Newton, on which you are standing, is one of several monadnocks in the Victoria vicinity. Like Mount Tolmie and Bear Hill, which are described in other chapters, Mount Newton withstood the weight and force of a 1500-m (5000-foot) thick ice sheet during the last period of glaciation. As the ice sheet moved it carried an immense load of rock, which blunted and rounded off the craggy outlines of Mount Newton.

At Pickles Bluff you will find another signpost, again for the Lauwelnew trail, which leads away from the bluff and inland toward the Coast Guard radar site. Travel this path and you will come to a gravel road. Bear left on the road until you come to a fork, at which you will bear right and head downhill on a Ministry of Transport road, which will take you back to the main parking lot.

HOW TO GET THERE: John Dean Park is located on Dean Park Road. Take Highway 17 to the East Saanich Road exit. Travel approximately 6 km (4 miles) north on East Saanich Road, to Dean Park Road. Turn left onto Dean Park Road and continue 4 km (2½ miles) to the parking lot.

14

Durrance Lake

MOUNT WORK REGIONAL PARK
HIGHLANDS

HIGHLIGHTS: Lake views, birdwatching, pond lilies, western white trillium

WALKING LEVEL: Easy; partially wheelchair accessible

SEASON: Early spring

ATTIRE: Regular

DOG WALKING: Excellent, but no dogs allowed June 1–September 15

ROUND TRIP: 2 km (1¼ miles)

DESIGNATED AS PARKLAND IN 1970, Mount Work offers many excellent hiking trails. It also provides a short and easy walk around the small and beautiful Durrance Lake. From the parking lot at the end of Durrance Close, a gravel trail begins by the Mount Work Regional Park sign and proceeds around the north side of the lake. This side of the lake is very easy walking because the path is wide and flat, and it can be negotiated by wheelchairs. It is also fairly dry, and on the land side of the trail you will see exposed patches of yellow-orange soil interspersed with stands of arbutus, grand fir, Douglas-fir and young maple. On the lake side, the soil is much moister and provides good growing conditions for cedar and salmonberry. Both these plant species were essential to the life of the aboriginal peoples: the cedar gave them shelter, clothing, tools, utensils and transportation, and the salmonberry served as food. Its tender young shoots were harvested in the early spring and eaten either raw or steamed.

The berries, which ripen from May through June, were often eaten with salmon, perhaps giving rise to the plant's name. Although many books describe them as insipid, with a tendency to mushiness, these

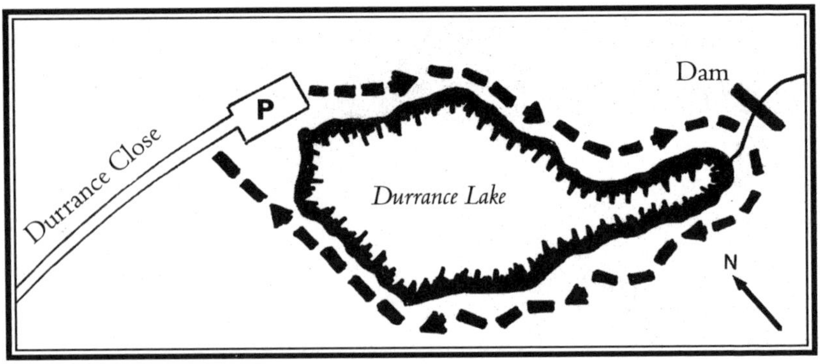

berries, like pale, flattened raspberries, are still a favourite with walkers. The tall, branching shrub has golden-brown shredding bark and alternate, deciduous, dark-green leaves, which make a perfect foil to the brilliant pink flowers that bloom from April to June. Their appearance coincides with the arrival of the rufous hummingbirds, and it is a treat to see several of these astonishing little birds dart about the salmonberry patches.

The path continues past a pure stand of red alder, indicating that the area may have been disturbed in some way. The red alder is a pioneer species and the first tree to appear after land has been logged or burnt. It is quick to invade and quick to grow, taking over a patch of land before the first Douglas-fir glimpses the light. As a result, foresters think of alders as weed trees, good only for firewood. They are, however, important nitrogen-fixing plants, like beans and peas, with the ability to extract nitrogen from the air. Nodules on their roots house an organism that converts the nitrogen into ammonium and nitrate, which are then released into the soil to be used by other plants. A stand of alders like this one can produce up to 320 kg (700 pounds) of nitrogen per year, giving the red alder an indispensable role in the regeneration of a forest.

About 300 m (1000 feet) from the start of the path you will come to a sandy beach—a good spot for picnics and swimming. Continue past the beach and you will see roundish holes in old snags, probably the work of hairy woodpeckers or flickers. You may also catch a fleeting glimpse of a Steller's jay, a flash of blue in the shadows, and you will probably hear its rasping cry in the distance. Ravens, which are common in the park, can be distinguished from crows by their wedge-shaped tails and much greater size. Their strange repertoire of yelps, barks, honks and caws is an eerie contrast to the general silence of the woods.

As you wind your way around the south side of Durrance Lake you are in a cedar and hemlock forest, and the contrast with the north side is extreme. Whereas the north side is sunny and open, the south side is dark and heavily forested, with trees growing right down to the the water's edge. About 100 m (330 feet) along, you will cross a small wooden bridge. Here the forest floor is open and strewn with fir needles, but as you walk on, the vegetation begins to fill in and become denser. Trailing blackberry weaves through sword ferns, leathery salal and the spiky-leafed Oregon grape, and Douglas-firs become more frequent.

The path now climbs by way of stone stairs. As you ascend, look along the border on the land side and find a true treasure of the West Coast forest, the western trillium. In early spring this plant bursts forth with a stalk bearing three large spade-shaped leaves, above which nestles the three-petalled white flower. The blooms appear in late March and often last well into May, turning a pink or purplish colour as they age, so that some people believe they are looking at a different species. This plant is classified as an "ant plant"—it relies on ants for seed dispersal. Attracted to the seeds, ants take them back to their nests. The seeds have an oil-rich appendage that the ants eat or feed to their larvae, after which they discard the seeds. In a dense forest, where seeds are not caught in the wind and blown to a new area, ant dispersal is vital to the western trillium's existence.

As you make your way toward the other end of Durrance Lake, you will cross a wooden bridge approximately 400 m (1300 feet) from the dam. A litter of blowdowns and drowned trees, probably caused by the artificial change in water level, provide a sheltered habitat for skunk cabbage, pond lilies and water grasses. This is the sort of place favoured by wood ducks, and in fact Durrance Lake is one of the most likely places to find these elegant and beautiful birds. Here they nest in old woodpecker holes and other cavities, usually at a considerable height. Upon hatching, the ducklings, unable to fly but weighing next to nothing, leap into space and tumble as much as 12 m (40 feet) to their mother, who waits below, calling encouragement. Quite unharmed by the fall, they follow her in single file to the nearest body of water.

At this end of the lake, the charred markings on the trunks of the Douglas-firs are evidence of past fires. Douglas-firs have exceptionally

Durrance Lake

thick bark that can resist a moderate forest fire. Other, less resistant, trees have succumbed, however, and pileated woodpeckers, flickers and hairy woodpeckers have moved in and made use of the burnt-out remains. The last section of the trail crosses a wooden bridge and ends 100 m (330 feet) beyond at Durrance Close, just before the parking lot. Walking back along the paved road, you will notice a sign warning that the dreaded Eurasian water milfoil is growing in Durrance Lake, as it is in other lakes mentioned in this book. This aquatic herb was introduced into North America in the late 1800s. With branching leafy shoots that house a myriad of leaves, this species replaces native communities of aquatic plants within three years.

HOW TO GET THERE: Durrance Lake is located at the end of Durrance Close. Take Highway 17 to the Royal Oak Drive turnoff. Travel west on Royal Oak to West Saanich Road. Turn right onto West Saanich, and follow it to Wallace Drive. Turn left onto Wallace Drive and follow it to Willis Point Road. Travel on Willis Point until you reach Durrance Close, where you turn right. The parking lot is at the end of Durrance Close.

15

McKenzie Bight

GOWLAND TOD PROVINCIAL PARK
HIGHLANDS

HIGHLIGHTS: Ferns, waterfowl, picnic spots, beach

WALKING LEVEL: Moderate

SEASON: All year

ATTIRE: Rainwear during winter

DOG WALKING: Excellent

ROUND TRIP: 3 km (2 miles)

IN 1994 VICTORIA HOSTED the Commonwealth Games, and in keeping with the spirit of this event the provincial and regional governments established the Commonwealth Nature Legacy to preserve a heritage of green space on southern Vancouver Island. One of the results has been the establishment of a 1200-ha (3000-acre) reserve called Gowlland Tod Provincial Park, which extends from the beginning of Finlayson Arm through Squally Reach to Saanich Inlet. The walk described in this chapter, the McKenzie Bight trail, is one of many in this park and one of the most beautiful.

From the McKenzie Bight parking lot, opposite the CRD Parks "McKenzie Bight" sign, a gravel path begins across the road. Be prepared—the only washrooms in the park are at the beginning of the trail, and the walk is a steady decline of 1.5 km (1 mile) down to the sea and then a constant equal incline back up the trail on the return trip. The walking is not difficult, but be cautious in the wet season because the terrain can be slippery.

At the beginning of the trail is a rich forest of Douglas-fir, bigleaf maple and red alder, with the usual understorey of salal and snowberry, as well as flowering currant. When it blooms in early April the currant is

McKenzie Bight

a strikingly ornamental shrub, with bright red, tubular flowers, which are a great attraction to rufous hummingbirds. At that time you are likely to see only male hummers, fiery chestnut and pugnacious; the green-backed females arrive a week or so later. By the time the currant bloom is over, males and females will be feeding side by side on the nectar of the orange honeysuckle.

The path winds downhill along the side of a ravine, where a profusion of ferns thrive in the moist conditions. Even in the dry days of summer the atmosphere here is one of damp greenness, reminding us of primeval days when tree ferns and giant horsetails dominated the swampy forests. The several kinds of ferns on the trail include delicate maidenhair, lady

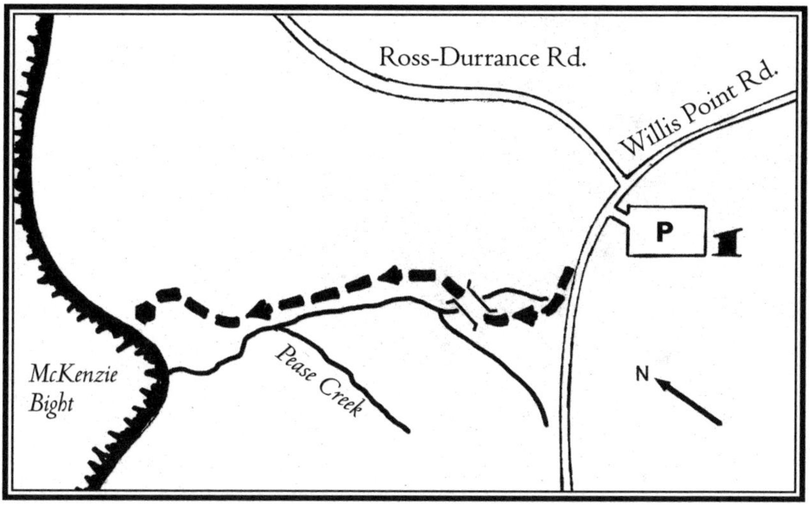

and licorice ferns, as well as the more robust bracken and the commonest species, the sword fern. This fern forms clumps of up to one hundred fronds, each about 60 cm (2 feet) long, sword-shaped and edged with rows of teeth—swords upon swords. The growing tip of each frond is rolled into a protective fiddlehead to prevent drying or breaking.

Ferns propagate not by seeds or flowers but by spores housed in spore cases on the underside of the fronds. Turn one over and you will see the double rows of orange-red spore cases, which, when dry, will burst and scatter their contents on the wind. One spore out of millions may land on moist ground and grow into a little heart-shaped plant containing both male and female organs. In the rain or on a film of dew, the male sperm is able to swim to and fertilize a female egg and so create a new fern. Once the fronds begin to grow, the little heart-shaped plant withers away.

As you climb down the trail you will see the scattered debris of fallen trees and broken boughs, evidence of past winter storms. Until quite recently foresters cut and removed deadwood of this kind, believing that it harboured noxious insects that were detrimental to the living trees. Now a more comprehensive view of forest life prevails, and it is understood that windfalls and snags provide essential shelter and food for the birds and small mammals whose presence is necessary to the well-being of the forest. Raccoons, squirrels and owls all breed in the cavities of dead trees, as do the woodpeckers, which hammer and drill in search of insects living under the flaking bark. White-faced hornets chew the decaying wood to build their paper nests, while innumerable other creatures and invisible organisms form the links of an essential chain of life that depends on the fallen trees.

More obvious to the eye is the vital role a dead tree plays in the life cycle of other plant life, both as host to lichens, mosses and fungi and as a nurse log to young plants. Broken down and digested by the lichens and fungi and by insects, the wood is converted into a fertile humus on which all the chance-blown seeds of the forest may germinate and grow.

Approximately 300 m (1000 feet) from the start of the trail, the path crosses McKenzie Creek and continues alongside it for the rest of the descent. Look at the plants bordering the path; they grow close to the ground and are easily missed because of their diminutive size, but they are worth a little attention. Heart-leaf spring beauty gives a lovely show of delicate five-petalled white flowers on 15-cm (6-inch) stems above its heart-shaped basal leaves. You should also be able to find foam flowers, vanilla leafs, star flowers, false Solomon's seal and miner's lettuce along the route. As you travel down this trail, look over to the far side of the ravine at the great stand of Douglas-firs and cedars. Often you can appreciate the size and grandeur of the trees more fully from a distance than when standing up close. Right beside the path, however, a beautiful grouping of three moss-covered maples, close at hand, have an interest that would be lost at a distance.

Further down the trail is an eroded area. Burlap and wire have been placed along the face of the banks for reinforcement, and wire cases of stones barricade the base of the trail to prevent slides. Soon you will come to the end of the forest and out onto McKenzie Bight beach. The bay, looking across to Squally Reach and the Malahat beyond, is particularly picturesque. On the stones and sandy mud of the beach American glasswort, or Pacific samphire, flourishes. This succulent plant has plump, cylindrical fleshy stems with distinct joints, rather like the scaly toes of a chicken, giving it the alternative name "chicken claws." Step on the stems and they burst with a crackling sound like breaking glass. Edible? Yes. Also known as "sea asparagus," this plant has become a favourite in chic restaurants as an accompaniment to seafood.

Great blue heron

On the right side of the bight there are rock outcrops overlooking the sea that provide wonderful spots for picnics or simply for resting before you face the climb back up the trail. Sitting at the water's edge you might catch sight of one of the resident belted kingfishers, whose antics when fishing can be extremely entertaining. Watch one of these handsome birds hover with fast-beating wings and downward-pointing bill as it searches the shallows for fish. Take time to sit quietly; you may hear the shrill calls of the bald eagles that roam the bay on the lookout for prey, or the hooting of a barred owl as it passes through to the wooded stretch of land to the left of the bay.

The bay has a serenity that is hard to part with when the time comes to walk back up the trail. Take your time on the return trip; your surroundings may appear quite different when seen from a new direction, and you will see things you missed on the way down.

HOW TO GET THERE: McKenzie Bight is located off Willis Point Road. Take Highway 17 to the Royal Oak Drive turnoff. Travel west on Royal Oak to West Saanich Road. Turn right onto West Saanich, following the road to Wallace Drive. Turn left onto Wallace Drive and follow it to Willis Point Road. Travel on Willis Point Road until you reach the McKenzie Bight parking lot on the left-hand side of the road.

16

Jocelyn Hill

GOWLLAND TOD PROVINCIAL PARK

HIGHLANDS

HIGHLIGHTS: Arbutus trees, wildflowers, mushrooms, vistas, picnic spots

WALKING LEVEL: Difficult

SEASON: Spring and autumn

ATTIRE: Sturdy walking shoes and rainwear during winter

DOG WALKING: Excellent

ROUND TRIP: 8 km (5 miles)

A NOTE OF WARNING: Jocelyn Hill is the most challenging walk in this book. Being quite long and steeper than most of the other walks, it could be classified as a hike. I include it here, however, because the trail is well maintained and because no part of it demands anything more than the ability to undertake a little arduous walking.

The Caleb Pike entrance to the park off Millstream Road is the only access to the south end of the Gowlland Range. The parking lot is large and has washrooms but no water. Just past the map board, a loose gravel path will take you to the trail markers and the beginning of the Jocelyn Hill trail. If you would like a shorter but more strenuous route, the Finlayson Arm Road trail provides a 3.8-km (2½-mile) round trip.

The first section of the Jocelyn Hill trail passes through a second-growth Douglas-fir forest. It is dry here, with shallow soil, and the trees tend to be spindly. The undergrowth consists of drought-tolerant plants like salal and Oregon grape. There also are saprophytes in this area—pine sap and Indian pipe, strange plants without chlorophyll that show their unusual, naked stalks in the middle of summer. After about 250 m (800 feet) the trail divides; keep on the main track, which is well marked with

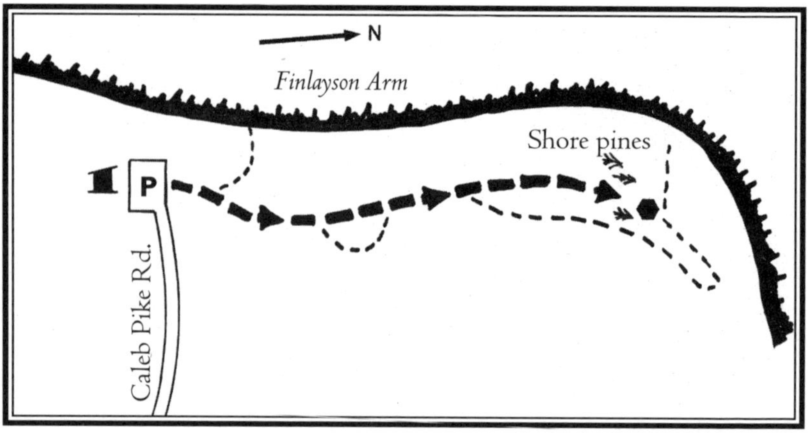

orange metal markers. A short distance further on you will come to a sign noting "Ridge Trail," an uphill path that is part of the Jocelyn Hill route. Follow this trail, where the loose gravel of the path has been replaced by compact earth. Take care while walking here; many rocks protrude above the trail surface to trip the unwary walker. Also, be careful not to be diverted onto any of the side trails. There are a number of them, and they should be ignored.

As you continue to climb you will start to see the distinctive red trunks of arbutus. The higher altitude, together with the dryness, are perfect conditions for these trees. Some other things to note along this trail are the wildflowers in spring and the mushrooms in fall. If you are climbing the trail in April or May keep your eyes open for the pink fairyslipper, a delicate orchid with a delicious perfume. Also known as ladyslippers or calypsos, fairyslippers are becoming rarer because of inadvertent trampling and especially because of thoughtless picking. They are strictly protected, so enjoy their beauty but please don't pick.

Another wildflower to watch for is the shooting star. Although this little plant is fairly common on the south coast and can be found on most of the trails described in this book, no other park can boast such a profusion of them as Jocelyn Hill. In the proper season, April and May, watch for their magenta-pink flowers dotting the first section of the walk. By the time you reach the hydro lines, under which the trail passes, the ground has become a carpet of these flowers. Take care not to stray from the path, because the habitat is extremely fragile and much unintended damage can be done to the plants at any time of the year. None should be picked.

A short way farther along the trail, you will come to a Jocelyn Hill kilometre marker indicating that you have another 3.1 km (2 miles) to travel to the lookout. About 200 m (650 feet) from the marker, you will come to a magnificent viewpoint looking over Finlayson Arm. A wide expanse of rock makes both a good resting spot for weary walkers and an excellent vantage point from which you may see soaring eagles and turkey vultures.

A further 500 m (1600 feet) brings you to another trail sign. Continue along the Ridge trail, which winds to the left, and keep your eyes open for the various types of mushrooms that appear in the damp days of fall. Each year produces a different variety of fungi. The more common mushrooms to watch for are the black helvella, with its lumpy, contorted greyish-black top, and the light brown, flat-topped poison paxillus, whose cap extends up to 12 cm (5 inches) wide. Both of these species are found near conifers. You will also spot deer mushrooms near decaying wood. This is a common fungus throughout North America and stands up to 11.5 cm (4½ inches) tall and 12.5 cm (5 inches) across. Its colour varies from dark brown to paler greyish-brown, depending on age.

The next section of the trail is a long, steep climb, but persevere and you will be rewarded by another trail sign telling you that it is only 1.8 km (1 mile) to the lookout. Here you will pass through a stand of shore pine, a highly adaptable tree species that can survive on windswept hilltops in soil that is low in nutrients. The climb continues, taking you past a large old Douglas-fir whose bark was blackened in patches by the heat of some past holocaust. Fires have probably ravaged this mountainside more than once, but the forest heals quickly, and as you look out across the expanse of green hillsides that make up the Gowlland Range there is little evidence of past destruction. This is true wilderness, where cougars roam and hunt, although you could live your whole life here and never see one. Shy and elusive, these great tawny cats lie up by day and become active only at twilight.

Just before reaching the lookout at Jocelyn Hill, you will come to a 200-m (650-foot) distance marker. You will have climbed quite high, as

View of Finlayson Arm from Jocelyn Hill

the vegetation nearby indicates. Look for the shrubs of hairy manzanita growing in this area. Often mistaken for dwarfed or young arbutus, this shrub is found where heat is most concentrated. The name is Spanish for "little apples" and refers to the shrub's edible fruit. From the marker the trail goes up and over a rock face, bringing you out onto a large clearing where the views are magnificent. On a clear day, the old cement works at Bamberton can be seen on the right and the inlet of Finlayson Arm on the left. The flat rock outcroppings in this area are perfect picnic or resting spots. When you are ready to head back, simply retrace your steps, making sure that you stay on the path marked with the orange metal markers.

HOW TO GET THERE: Jocelyn Hill is located off Caleb Pike Road. Take Highway 1 west to Millstream Road. Turn right onto Millstream Road and proceed to Caleb Pike Road. Turn left onto Caleb Pike and follow it to the park entrance, a short distance along.

17

Lone Tree Hill Regional Park

HIGHLANDS

HIGHLIGHTS: Arbutus trees, vistas, wildflowers

WALKING LEVEL: Difficult

SEASON: Spring

ATTIRE: Rainwear for wet weather

DOG WALKING: Excellent

ROUND TRIP: 2 km (1¼ miles)

ONE OF THE MANY pleasures of walking in and around Victoria is the show of spring wildflowers that bloom from early March to the end of July. Many of these flowers grow in association with Garry oaks and arbutus, so they occur on hillsides where the ground is drier. Lone Tree Hill offers a short walk through just such a habitat, with an outstanding display of native wildflowers in season. The loose-gravel trail can be slippery during wet weather, and the walk is a bit of a climb. However, it is a short walk, approximately 1 km (⅔ mile) to the top, and there are many places to rest along the way, with exceptional views.

The trail begins winding through a forest of western red cedars and Douglas-firs with ocean spray, flowering currant, Oregon grape and salal. In an area that is relatively dry, this is the dampest part. Look for the bright orange, red and yellow blooms of the western columbine, one of the most beautiful wildflowers around. Take the time to examine a blossom head; the petals are spurred at one end, joined near midlength to a floral ring of sepals, and delicately flared above, with protruding tufted stamens and style. The splash of colour in the green forest sends a signal to the hummingbirds and insects that sustenance is to be had.

The trail continues up and out of the forest, now winding over more open ground, where moss-covered outcroppings of rock border the path. This is raven country, and as you emerge from the trees into the open you will hear their barking voices all around you. On the right side of the trail, not more than 400 m (1300 feet) from the start, sits a large rock, which, in the middle of April, is cloaked in the pink blooms of sea blush. This small annual, standing 10–60 cm (4–24 inches) tall, finds sufficient moisture in the thin covering of mosses to thrive and spread.

In and about this same area the first arbutus appears. This is the only broad-leaved evergreen tree native to Canada and is restricted to the southern half of Vancouver Island along the Strait of Georgia and south to Washington, Oregon and California. In the United States it is also known as a Pacific madrone, a name given to it by the early Spanish explorers. *Madroño* is the Spanish word for the arbutus's close relative, the Mediterranean strawberry tree, which tells you something of the type of climate—hot and dry—that the arbutus prefers. It is probably one of the easiest trees in our area to identify because of its distinctive bark.

As the arbutus tree grows, the thin, satiny-smooth, reddish-brown bark peels away, exposing the new olive- or lime-green bark underneath. The trunk is usually short and the branches often crooked or twisted, although the tree may reach a height of 30 m (100 feet). The leaves are oval and thick, shiny green on top and pale dull-green below. Dense clusters of urn-shaped, waxy white flowers appear in April and May and have a strong, sweet odour that is very attractive to bees. Bright orange-red berries form during the summer, maturing in September. Arbutus is a pioneer plant that moves in when a space becomes available. It is not, however, particularly tolerant of shade, so it establishes itself in clearings and on open rocky bluffs. When climbing Lone Tree Hill, you will see both these types of habitat.

As you approach the last leg of your uphill journey, you will travel a series of short switchbacks. This section is challenging but short-lived. Watch for a side trail leading to a lookout just after the end of the switchbacks. Even if you do not need an excuse to rest, the views of the Sooke

Arbutus tree

Red columbine

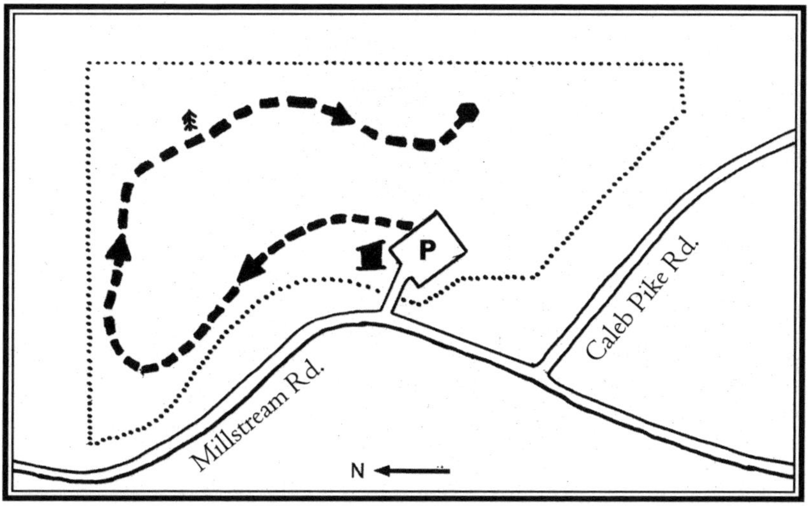

Hills are worth the stop, and if you are here in spring, the immediate surroundings are carpeted with flowers.

In May, look for the pale-yellow blooms of death camas. This is a perennial bulb that stands up to 60 cm (24 inches) tall and grows on forest edges, rocky or grassy slopes and often among common camas in damp meadows. It differs from the common camas, however, in being highly poisonous. The aboriginal people who harvested the bulb of the common camas were well aware of death camas and took great care not to harvest the wrong bulb. In time, the death camas bulbs were weeded out of blue camas beds to make harvesting easier and safer. Distinguishing between the two species is made simpler by the overlapping of their blooming season, although common camas begins to show blue a few weeks before the yellow flowers of death camas appear.

Many other wildflowers adorn the slopes of Lone Tree Hill. (At the lookout I have counted seventeen species of wildflowers within a square foot.) Wild strawberries, shooting stars and fairy slippers are only a few of the many that adorn this hill. Earlier in the season, before these others appear, watch for fawn lilies and the small-flowered, blue-eyed Mary and spring gold.

The trail continues, passing another offshoot to yet another lookout. As you ascend Lone Tree Hill the views become even more extensive, with a 360-degree panorama at the top. On a clear day you will be able to see the Olympic Mountains across Juan de Fuca Strait, the skyline of Victoria, and the mountains and hilltops of Saanich. Looking down directly to the east you will see several lakes, part of the series of lakes that lie in the Highlands. The summit is not a place for the fainthearted, and young children should be closely supervised because the top is a pinnacle with few ledges. Before heading back, take a moment to look at the lone fir tree—or, more precisely, the lone fir tree stump—the namesake of the park, which stands at the top of the summit. This short, wizened tree is over two hundred years old. Its appearance is a reminder of the harsh conditions endured by the flora on this windswept hill.

To return to the parking lot, retrace your steps, being especially cautious on the steeper parts of the trail. Keep an eye out as you make your way down the hill for the expansive and handsome arbutus trees. It is amazing how much you can miss while walking uphill, and you are likely to find your return journey down as rewarding and full of interest as the trip up.

HOW TO GET THERE: Lone Tree Hill Park is located on Millstream Road. Take Highway 1 west to the Langford–Millstream Road exit, about 10 km (6 miles) from downtown Victoria. Turn right onto Millstream Road and stay on it almost until the end, where you will find a large CRD sign and parking lot. A word of warning: Do not take Millstream Lake Road, which branches off Millstream Road, and beware of the road sign for Lone Tree Hill Park that appears 200 m (660 feet) before the park and has an arrow pointing right. Do not turn off Millstream Road, but go straight on and you will find the park.

18

Francis / King Regional Park

SAANICH

HIGHLIGHTS: Nature house, old-growth forest, fungi, wildflowers

WALKING LEVEL: Easy to moderate

SEASON: Spring and autumn

ATTIRE: Rainwear during wet months, and sturdy walking shoes

DOG WALKING: Excellent, but dogs must be kept on a leash

ROUND TRIP: 2 km (1¼ miles)

IF YOU WANT TO walk in an authentic old-growth forest, Francis/King Regional Park is the place to go. An amalgamation of Thomas Francis Park and Freeman King Park, it lies in the heart of Saanich and offers 91 ha (225 acres) of wilderness, which includes some the largest Douglas-firs in the Victoria area. This well-loved park is frequented by local people but does not attract many out-of-town visitors, though few parks in the region can boast the beauty of Francis/King. The Elsie King trail, a wheelchair-accessible boardwalk path, offers people with limited mobility the chance to enjoy the beauty of a woodland walk. Temporarily closed, it was extended and reopened in 1999 with new interpretive signs.

The walk described below winds through what is classified by plant biologists as the coastal Douglas-fir zone, one of the fourteen zones in British Columbia. On Vancouver Island two zones predominate, coastal Douglas-fir and coastal western hemlock; these are further subdivided into subzones or ecosystems, which are determined on the basis of regional differences in climate. Victoria lies in the coastal Douglas-fir zone, but the variety of sites within the area produces many different associations of plants and animals. A walk through Francis/King park provides a good sample of the various combinations possible in one major zone. In the moist, low-lying areas, western red cedars, grand firs, bigleaf maples and western flowering dogwoods occur in conjunction with understorey plants such as sword fern, salmonberry and trillium. The wetter, swampier parts of the park are home to red alder, Indian plum and skunk cabbage. Partway up the wooded slopes, where the forest is dry and the soil shallow, the Douglas-fir is accompanied by a wiry undergrowth of Oregon grape and salal. Even further up the dry rock outcrops, Garry oak and arbutus are found with wild rose, snowberry and ocean spray.

Cross Munn Road from the parking lot and pick up a gravel trail that leads to a turnstile, where a signpost marks the beginning of Centennial trail, a compact dirt path. This will take you downhill under a canopy of large, moss-covered bigleaf maples and Garry oaks, whose limbs are festooned with lichens. Early-flowering Indian plum and the heavily scented, yellow blossoms of the maples make this part of the walk particularly appealing in early spring.

As the path continues, the forest becomes damper and more and more western red cedars and young western hemlocks appear among the Douglas-firs, a reminder that the coastal western hemlock zone lies right next door, in the Sooke Hills. As you stand on the trail, all around you is green, a green so pervasive and complete that it seems a quality of the light. Chartreuse green are the ferns springing from the forest floor, grey-green the lichens on the cedars and emerald the mosses. Green of every shade and intensity is here.

There is a rich organic presence in this woodland, and everywhere communities of plants and animals live in an interdependent harmony that can be broken by the least alteration in its balance. As you pass the stump of a fallen tree, stop and examine it. Mosses and lichens have claimed its surface, trapping moisture and supporting a multitude of organisms, hardly any bigger than a small spider. On the stump's broken top, seeds have lodged and forest plants are growing. Some, like the licorice ferns sprouting from fissures in the wood, are small. Others, like the hemlock seedlings, will be giants and send great root tentacles to embrace and eventually devour their nursery.

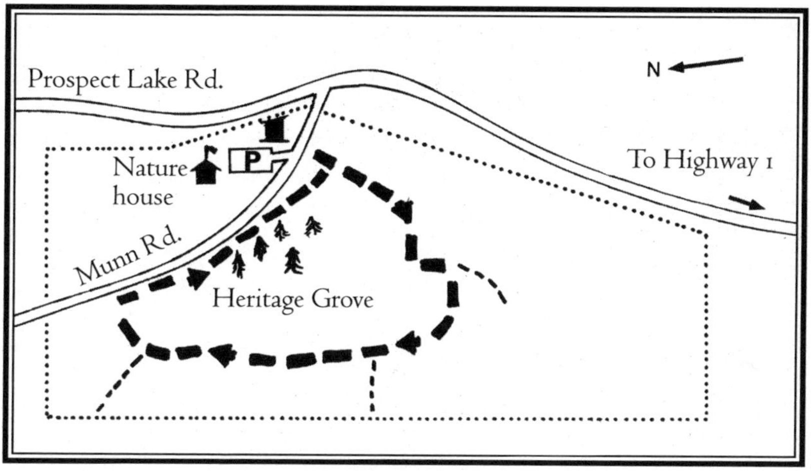

Keep your ears open for the dry, intermittent croak of the Pacific tree frog. This is a common amphibian, ranging in colour from brown to bronze to green to grey, but it is often missed because of its ability to blend into its surroundings. The conspicuous discs on its toes and the dark bands on its cheeks make it easy to distinguish the Pacific tree frog from others found in the area.

As the trail continues, it winds through an area where charred Douglas-firs indicate the ravages of some past fire. Wildfires were once common in the coastal Douglas-fir zone and played an important role in shaping its ecosystems. Old Douglas-firs have thick bark that protects them from all but the hottest flames, and one reason why this species predominates is its resistance to fire. The old trees survive, and after a fire the seedlings quickly colonize the blackened area in which less fire-resistant species have been killed.

Continuing along the path, you will come to another sign marking the Centennial trail. Stay on this trail and cross a small stream. About 100 m (330 feet) on, bear right at the next signpost, staying on Centennial trail. There are exposed roots in this section of the route, so be careful. Here western red cedars are numerous and the undergrowth sparse. This is a wet area, in which a high water table leads to shallow tree roots and frequent blowdowns. The forest floor is strewn with the debris of countless seasons of growth and decay and is perfect mushroom habitat. One

Burnt hollow of a western red cedar

species you may see in autumn is the pale-grey oyster mushroom, growing quite visibly in large clusters on fallen wood. Cross a small bridge about 100 m (330 feet) down the trail and look for an attractive little fungus growing on fallen branches or rain-soaked stumps. Its bright yellow or orange colour and gelatinous texture suggest its common name, witch's butter. Try to find the odd-looking, grey mushroom known as elf's saddle, with its saddle-shaped cap. It comes to fruit from late spring through autumn and occurs singly or in scattered groups.

If you pass a fallen maple, keep an eye open for the ghoulishly named dead man's fingers growing in clusters, often at soil level. It is easy to miss; its black colour and rounded club tips blend into the background of rotting wood and damp soil in the forest. Most of these fungi appear in autumn, but in spring look for the common morel, with its tawny-brown, honeycomb-like head. To those who know their mushrooms, it is a table delicacy. Quite another matter is the deadly poisonous fly agaric, found in late summer and early fall, often near Douglas-fir trees. The arrestingly beautiful orange or red cap with speckles of white is a warning that this is one mushroom better looked at from afar.

After about 200 m (650 feet), you will come to a sign marking the trail to Thetis Lake park. This connector trail joins Francis/King with both Thetis Lake and Mill Hill parks. The three-park corridor provides the ambitious walker with a long and beautiful route. Keep on Centennial trail, however, and you will cross a wooden bridge with another sign marking a side trail to Munn Road. If you wish to shorten your route, take this trail. It is an easy walk via the road and will return you to Francis/King parking lot and the nature house. A number of other small trails lead to Munn Road from Centennial trail, any of which may be used to curtail the route described here.

Approximately 200 m (650 feet) further along, you will come to a park boundary sign. Stay on the main trail, which starts to travel uphill. The ascent is short but steep and takes you over bare rock outcrops, which can be slippery after a rainfall. With the change in elevation and the correspondingly much drier conditions, the vegetation alters substantially and you enter a new ecosystem that is home to the Garry oak and the arbutus. In dry sites with well-drained soil, these trees form an open cover above a carpet of grasses and spring wildflowers. Look for the white petals of the fawn lily in early spring or the blue of camas flowers one or two months later. Once the trail has reached the top, it descends and once again you pass through groves of cedar and Douglas-fir. About 350 m (1150 feet) down you will come to a sign marking the Grand Fir trail. Take this path, and in about 200 m (650 feet) you will come to Heritage Grove. Here stand 500-year-old Douglas-firs more than 80 m (250 feet) tall, their trunks over 3 m (10 feet) in diameter.

When you leave Heritage Grove, take the unmarked trail to the left. This will lead you back to Centennial trail after about 150 m (500 feet). You are now back in the wetter part of the park, where skunk cabbage and sword ferns thrive among the mosses. About 300 m (1000 feet) further on, the trail recrosses the same wooden bridge that you encountered on the first half of the walk and retraces the route back to the parking lot.

Before leaving Francis/King park, take the time to meander through the nature house. Its displays are well presented, and the volunteer

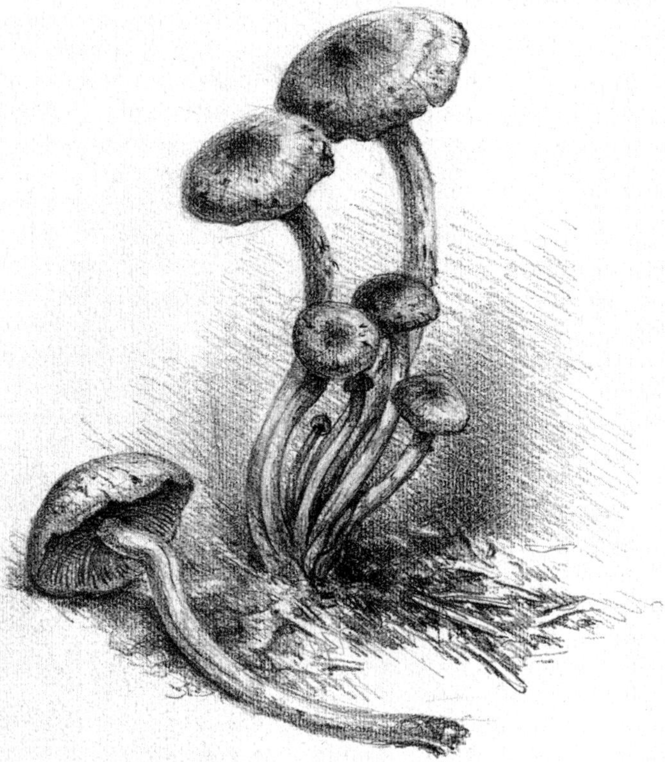

Sulfur tuft

naturalists on hand are interesting to talk to and knowledgeable about the park's natural history.

HOW TO GET THERE: Francis/King Regional Park is located on Munn Road. Follow Highway 1 to Helmcken Road. Turn north onto Helmcken, left onto Burnside Road West, and right onto Prospect Lake Road. Follow Prospect Lake Road to Munn Road. The parking lot and nature house are located on Munn Road.

19

Upper Thetis Lake

THETIS LAKE REGIONAL PARK
VIEW ROYAL

HIGHLIGHTS: Lake views, swimming, birdwatching, arbutus, cedar, and Douglas-fir forest

WALKING LEVEL: Easy to moderate

SEASON: All year

ATTIRE: Sturdy walking shoes and rainwear for rainy months

DOG WALKING: Good

ROUND TRIP: 3 km (2 miles)

ONE OF THE MOST beautiful and diverse natural parks in the Victoria area is Thetis Lake Regional Park. Encompassing two lakes, Upper and Lower Thetis, and offering many walking and hiking trails, this 635-ha (1569-acre) park is the perfect choice for those who would like a longer journey. The walk described in this chapter follows a circular path around Upper Thetis Lake.

There is a small charge for parking in either of the two lots; try the second parking lot, where the trail begins, but if it is full, park in the main lot and walk to the trailhead. At first the path is paved, but it soon becomes compact dirt. At a branch in the trail about 50 m (165 feet) further on, take the left-hand, narrower, path over a stone bridge and you will come to a turnstile and a "Walker" sign. Walk through the turnstile and enjoy a view of the lake. Originally just one lake, Upper Thetis and Lower Thetis were divided by a small dike to provide access for a fire road from one side of the lake to the other. A large culvert was installed in the middle of the dike to link the two lakes. Today, under the management of the Capital Regional District, these two deep, clear lakes provide much enjoyment to those who wish to walk, hike, canoe, swim or fish.

The Upper Thetis Lake trail weaves through a typical coast forest ecosystem, which has three distinct plant associations: hemlock–cedar, Douglas-fir, and oak–arbutus. Each of these zones has its own plants, animals and birds and is governed by a particular combination of altitude, temperature and rainfall. Hemlock–cedar predominates in the wettest parts, and the Douglas-fir association is located in the drier areas. Even drier country is preferred by oak and arbutus, which generally are found where annual rainfall is less than 25 cm (10 inches). Typically salal is found with Douglas-fir and sword ferns with cedar, but things are not always so precisely arranged, nor are the plant zones so clearly demarcated. More often a forest will be in transition, exhibiting a blend of forest types. For example, at Upper Thetis Lake the first part of the trail leads through a mixed wood of Douglas-fir and maple. Here the undergrowth of salal, bitter cherry, salmonberry and ferns is fairly dense.

Two hundred metres (650 feet) along, the path starts to climb to a drier area, where trees become spindly, the forest more open and the undergrowth sparser. Travel down the path to the lake's edge, where moisture-loving plants find conditions to their liking. Here, emerging directly from the dank ground, are the exaggerated leaves of the skunk cabbage, whose great, golden sheaths provide splashes of colour in the dark forest in March and April. The faintly repellent methane odour that gives this plant its common name is as characteristic of the forest as the trees themselves.

Among the Douglas-firs on the land side of the trail is a stand of western red cedars. Happy in the damp conditions of the lakeside, these trees block the sunlight with their huge boughs, threatening to smother the Douglas firs. It is difficult to think of fire as a necessary element in the regeneration of a forest, but it is essential to the life cycle of many plants, including Douglas-firs. To germinate, their seeds must have sunlight, virtually unknown in a mature cedar grove unless fire clears a space. If this does not happen, fallen Douglas-firs will be replaced, not by others of their kind, but by red cedars.

One of the truly beautiful features of this walk is the exposed rock left over from an earlier glacial age. Particularly on the wetter parts of the trail, the rock is covered with a rich blanket of moss, brilliant green and spongy. Soil and nutrients trapped in the water-retentive mass provide

Upper Thetis Lake

good conditions for some types of wildflowers, and in summer this is where you may see the delicate pale-pink bells of the twin-flowers growing among the wiry-stemmed salal, Oregon grape and sword ferns.

About 300 m (1000 feet) along the trail, you will come across evidence of woodpecker activity—rough excavations in the rotting, orange wood of decayed stumps and snags. The larger, oval diggings are the work of pileated woodpeckers and have been hacked out by the powerful bills of these great, crow-sized birds as they search for grubs and boring insects. With their flaming red crests and black-and-white plumage, pileated woodpeckers are striking in every way and utterly typical of the

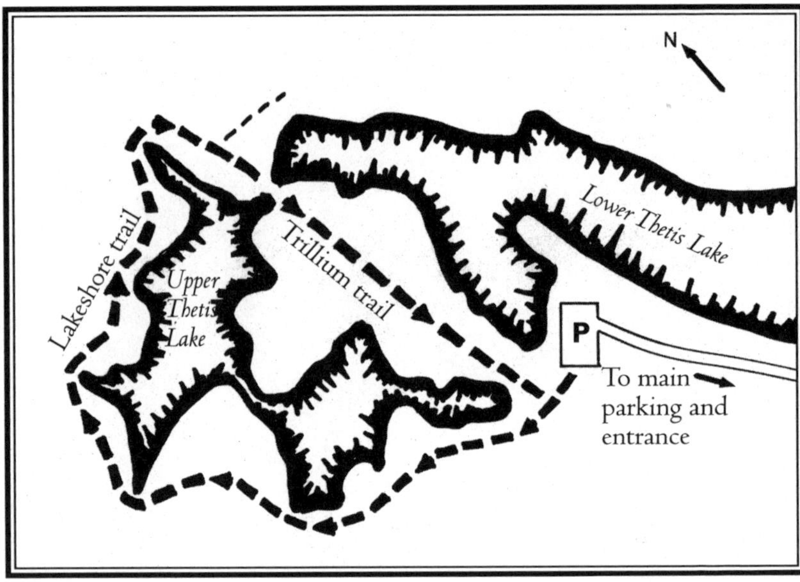

coniferous forest. You cannot spend much time in these surroundings without hearing their ringing cries or, in spring, the staccato drumming of the males in courtship. There are smaller, rounder holes too, made by hairy woodpeckers. Neither the oval nor the round excavations should be confused with the nesting cavities that woodpeckers make, usually high above the forest floor.

A woodpecker hole of any kind is usually recognizable, but more puzzling may be the rows of small, square perforations that sometimes encircle the trunks of trees. These have been made by red-breasted sapsuckers, small woodpeckers that drink the sap flowing from the shallow, regular depressions. Moths and other insects are also attracted to the sweet liquid and become an additional source of food for the sapsuckers.

The path continues to a drier area where one side of the trail is banked by a large rock face, which offers a rich assortment of wildflowers throughout the growing season. In early spring, look for satin flowers and white fawn lilies. As the last of the lilies dries and turns inward, the buds of the shooting stars begin to unfold. Soon afterward, cushions of seablush appear, followed by the brilliant yellow flowers of the stonecrop.

Just a short distance down the trail, the path leads to a rock outcrop overlooking the lake. Here a bench with a spectacular view of the lake awaits the weary walker. This is one of the many choice spots for lookouts and picnics on this section of the trail. From here, you can see an arm of land projecting into the lake and forming a sheltered backwater for ducks and other waterfowl. The trail descends to the water's edge and winds through the forest, coming to a wooden bridge. Several subsidiary tracks branch from the main trail, but if in doubt about which way to go, keep along the lake. Quite soon after the wooden bridge, the trail reaches the farthest bend in the lake and crosses another bridge.

Take a moment to look at the life around the creek that flows under the bridge and into the lake. In summer, dragonflies hover above the water while butterflies alight on the white blossoms of the Pacific ninebark, the red-osier dogwoods or the dusty-pink blooms of hardhack or spirea that grow in profusion around the bridge. The nitrogen-fixing alders provide this bank of vegetation with rich nutrients, and the atmosphere is lush, damp and green. Mosquitoes, too, find the lakeside a congenial place to breed, so on warm evenings you may not wish to linger. If you do, you will be rewarded in May and June by a concert of olive-backed thrushes, whose fluting, ethereal song is one of the pleasures of summer.

With gentle undulations, the trail begins the driest section of the walk, where the inward side of the path is ornamented by the peeling red trunks of arbutus. After climbing up and away from the creek, watch for a secondary trail that diverges from the main path and leads to a lookout above the lake, well worth the short walk. Along the main path the forest becomes an interesting mix of vegetation. The up-and-down of the trail gives alternating patterns of arbutus, salal and ocean spray in the higher, drier sections, and alders, little-leaved buttercups and avens in the lower, wetter areas.

About 150 m (500 feet) from the last major lookout, the trail forks. Stay along the lakeside (the right branch) until you come to a creek bed, where an alternative walk, the McKenzie Creek trail, joins the main path. If you choose to stay on the main trail, the landmark to watch for is the magnificent rock face on the land side of the trail. Completely exposed to the elements and not sheltered by forest, the spring wildflowers growing here, such as camas and spring gold and the orange-blooming maconella of summer, must rely on a crusty layer of lichen and moss to support them. After passing through a dense stand of conifers and deciduous trees, the trail ascends and the forest starts to thin.

You will now be coming to the last stage before heading back along the fire road. Watch closely, because there is another fork, which leads to the Lower Thetis Lake trail. If you stay on the main path, take the time to admire the exceptional view it affords of Upper Thetis Lake. The path passes over a bare rock outcrop often used by picnickers and continues for about another 100 m (330 feet) before coming to a turnstile. Pass through this to reach the fire road, turn right and you will soon find yourself back at the car park.

HOW TO GET THERE: Thetis Lake Regional Park is located off Six Mile Road. Take Highway 1 west to the Colwood exit and turn onto Highway 1A. From Highway 1A turn right onto Six Mile Road, and continue straight ahead to the park entrance and the main parking lot. Continue past this lot and turn left to reach the second parking lot.

20

Goldstream Provincial Park

LANGFORD

HIGHLIGHTS: Salmon spawning, birdwatching, visitors' centre, estuary, salamanders, picnic area

WALKING LEVEL: Easy; partially wheelchair accessible

SEASON: Late autumn to early winter

ATTIRE: Rainwear during autumn and winter

DOG WALKING: Dogs must be on a leash at all times

ROUND TRIP: 2 km (1¼ miles)

WHERE TO WALK ON a rainy day? This is an important question, since for at least half the year the skies above Victoria can be relied upon to bring showers or steady downpours. One answer is to go to Goldstream, which in many ways is at its best in wet weather. This is a beautiful park, where stands of giant cedars and magnificent maples provide a canopy dense enough to protect walkers from at least a slight drizzle. If the rain becomes a deluge, an exceptional visitors' centre offers shelter and, at the same time, information about the park's natural history. Goldstream is also a major spawning ground for three of the five species of Pacific salmon. Every autumn, it offers visitors one of the most moving and impressive spectacles on the northwest coast.

On arriving at Goldstream, park in the first parking lot if possible or, if you cannot, park further along and walk back to the first lot. Look for a gravel trail, starting at the picnic area, that runs parallel to the river. This is Riverside trail and, although there is no sign marking the path, it

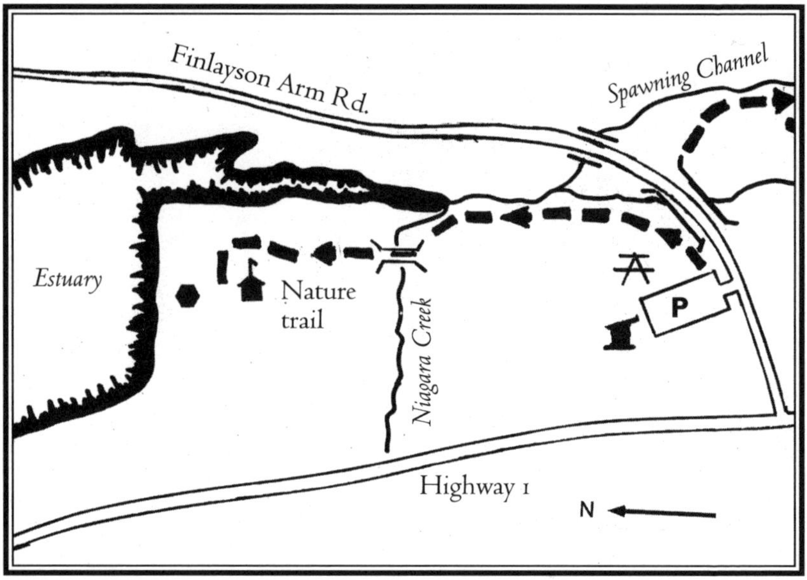

is easy to find. It is wide, flat and well maintained, making it suitable for wheelchair users.

The trail winds its way to the bank of the Goldstream River and continues beside the water to end at the visitors' centre on the estuary. Before reaching the centre, the trail crosses three metal bridges from which you can take a good look into the river as it passes below. In autumn they are ideal viewpoints from which to watch the salmon as they rest in the eddies and backwaters formed by tangles of sticks and grasses.

The energy required to fuel a salmon on its journey from the sea to its breeding ground is astonishing, but once it reaches fresh water, the salmon does not feed again. How it finds its way to its parent stream is a mystery of navigation, a source of wonder and admiration. Chum are the salmon you are most likely to see, because this is the most abundant species in the river. Male chums are a murky grey-green, often with reddish vertical bars, whereas the females are a creamy grey, with a dark midstripe running the length of each side. Walk quietly, and take a few minutes to watch. You will see great salmon working their way upstream, their strength nearly spent, in water barely deep enough to contain them. You may also see pairs digging and defending their nests in the gravel beds where they spawn.

Estuary at Goldstream

To make the nest, the female turns on her side and repeatedly lifts her tail violently away from the gravel. This dislodges the gravel, which the current carries downstream. To test the depth of the resulting trench or nest, the female arches her body in a U shape and feels for the bottom of the stream with her anal fins. When the trench is deep enough, she moves over it and deposits her eggs, or roe. After standing guard while the trench was made, the male quickly moves in to fertilize the eggs with a shower of white sperm, or milt. There may well be a second male waiting to fertilize the roe, because chum salmon do not pair absolutely.

Once the eggs have been fertilized the female digs upstream, shifting the gravel down over the nest to protect the eggs. After spawning is complete, both the male and female salmon die, their purpose accomplished and their strength exhausted. Their dead carcasses, thousands of them, litter the shallows and the banks of the stream, providing an annual feast

Goldstream River

for gulls, eagles, raccoons, mink and many other animals. In a few weeks, nothing is left except a few desiccated skeletons.

Just past the third bridge you will come to a "quiet zone" area, which is a prime birdwatching spot. Several kinds of gulls can be seen feeding on the dead salmon, such as mew gulls, herring gulls, Thayer's gulls, occasional glaucous gulls and, of course, the more common glaucous-winged gulls. The bald eagle is another bird attracted to the salmon carcasses, and one of the excitements of coming to Goldstream at spawning time is to see the great number of eagles, sometimes dozens together, feeding or perched on the surrounding trees like Christmas ornaments.

A particularly interesting bird to watch for at any time of the year is the dipper, robin-sized, plump and greyish, which bobs up and down with its tail flicked upward. Others, such as the belted kingfisher and the great blue heron, are also year-round inhabitants and may be seen fishing in the quiet zone. Although you will not see one, the marbled murrelet, the little seabird whose nesting habits were a deep mystery to scientists until recently, is now known to breed in the old-growth forest in Goldstream.

The trail continues through a thickly forested section, where large cedars grace the way. This is a damp region of sword ferns, good habitat for the western red-backed salamander. In fact, Goldstream has the greatest concentration of these salamanders in the world. If you want to see one of these little creatures, you may have to search carefully under rotting logs or in the middle of a clump of sword ferns. The broad reddish or yellowish band down the length of its back distinguishes the western red-backed from other salamanders.

The path crosses a wooden bridge over Niagara Creek, and then goes on to the estuary, where the visitors' centre stands. Before going into the centre, take the time to walk the short distance to a birdwatching platform at the edge of the estuary. This is the farthest point you are allowed to walk. The estuary has been closed to the public for several years, and as a result the number of visiting bald eagles has grown substantially. Even black bears occasionally make their way down to the water to feed undisturbed by people. As you leave the platform look up at Mount Finlayson, which stands on the far side of Goldstream. This is an impressive sight, and its close proximity makes it appear to tower to a great height.

Next stop is the Freeman King Visitors' Centre, a delightful place to spend an hour. There is an exceptionally good natural-history bookstore in the centre, and the displays about the fauna and flora of the park are both informative and fun. You can also learn about the geology of the park and how the melting of the great ice sheets of the last glacial period left Goldstream and the estuary in their wake.

The route continues back the way you came, or if you wish to cut short your journey, you can take the path leading directly to the parking lot instead of retracing Riverside trail. If you are interested in the spawning channel, continue to the green bridge just beyond the first parking lot. This bridge crosses the Goldstream River at the start of Finlayson Arm Road. Just beyond it, look for a compact dirt trail running to the right. This path, Bridge trail, although it is easy and short, is not wheelchair accessible. It will take you down to a stream that has been diverted from the main river to create a spawning channel. Wooden boards are

Dipper

used to control the depth and rate of flow of the stream to assist the salmon as they move upstream.

This is a quiet spot where, at the right time of the year, you may spot coho spawning. Coho prefer tiny tributaries but tend to be shy, often hiding beneath logs. Look for the brightly coloured dark-green heads and bright-red sides of the males and the similar, but less vibrant, markings of the females. The coho do not return to Goldstream every year. Although in some years they arrive in healthy numbers, in other years they are extremely scarce. Another species of salmon seen in the spawning channel is the chinook or spring. This is a larger salmon, purplish-black in colour, with dark spots. Its numbers have been increasing over the years, probably owing to recently completed stream improvements.

The Bridge trail is a short 150 m (500 feet) to the beginning of the channel diversion, at which spot you can turn and retrace your steps to the bridge and the parking lot.

HOW TO GET THERE: Take Highway 1 west; the park entrance is a right turn off the highway, 19 km (12 miles) from downtown Victoria.

21

Mill Hill Regional Park

LANGFORD

HIGHLIGHTS: Garry oak and arbutus forest, wildflowers, rock striations, vistas

WALKING LEVEL: Difficult

SEASON: Late winter to early summer

ATTIRE: Sturdy walking shoes

DOG WALKING: Excellent

ROUND TRIP: 2 km (1¼ miles)

HAVE YOU SEEN THE wildflowers on Mill Hill? If not, then this is a walk you should take, for Mill Hill in spring is one of Victoria's most beautiful sights. Before beginning your walk, visit the CRD headquarters, reached from the parking lot by a short trail. The headquarters offers informative brochures, and to help guide your walk, pick up a copy of the brochure *Wildflowers of Mill Hill.* The few minutes spent perusing the list before starting out will add to your pleasure.

Look for the Calypso trailhead at the far end of the parking lot. It is a wide path through an old, mixed forest, where you will see large cedars, Douglas-firs, grand firs, and even western hemlock. After walking about 50 m (165 feet), you will cross the CRD Headquarters road and pick up the trail on the other side. This well-marked path continues down an attractive ravine to the bottom, into which Mill Stream trickles. In early spring the ravine is where you will see the stately trillium flowers, their triangular splashes of white brightening the

Start of Calypso trail

otherwise dark forest. They should not be picked, either here in the park or anywhere else.

After walking down about 100 m (330 feet) you will come to the Calypso trail sign. Bear right at this sign and you will start to travel uphill, on the way passing the CRD headquarters. Keep an eye out for the strictly protected provincial tree, the western flowering dogwood, and its creamy blossoms. This tree prefers well-drained slopes and may grow to 9 m (30 feet) in height. More often, however, it is found as a bushy shrub of less than 3 m (10 feet). The flowers appear from April through June and again in September and consist of greenish knobs, each surrounded by four to six white bracts, which look like petals.

As you climb, the walk will become more difficult; loose stones and protruding roots are common. A short way along, the Calypso intersects with the Auburn trail, an alternative route from the parking lot. Stay on

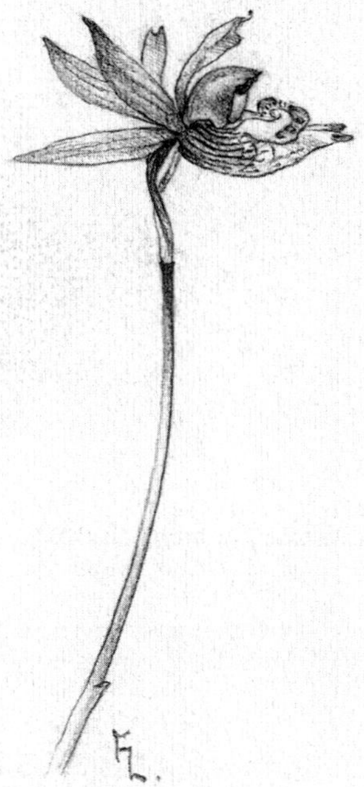

Fairy slipper

Calypso, which continues up the hill in a steep climb. A short way along, the path forms into switchbacks. Although the trail's steepness makes it challenging, the path itself is in good condition. As you walk the switchbacks keep an eye open for the tiny, scented flower that is the trail's namesake, *Calypso bulbosa,* or fairy slipper. This little pink orchid flowers from April to June and is a wonderful distraction from the arduous climb. It is hard to see at first because its subtlety and diminutive size cause it to be easily missed. Once you spot one, however, you will begin to see a veritable carpet of these little treasures.

As you travel up the hill, you will notice the change in vegetation. The large conifers of the forest below are replaced by Garry oaks and arbutus. This is the dry side of Mill Hill, and the trees are spindly and short. Among the Garry oaks and rocky outcroppings are patches of deeper soil, good spots for the white fawn lilies. The Easter lily, as it is also known, appears early, preceded in March by its mottled, glossy leaves. By

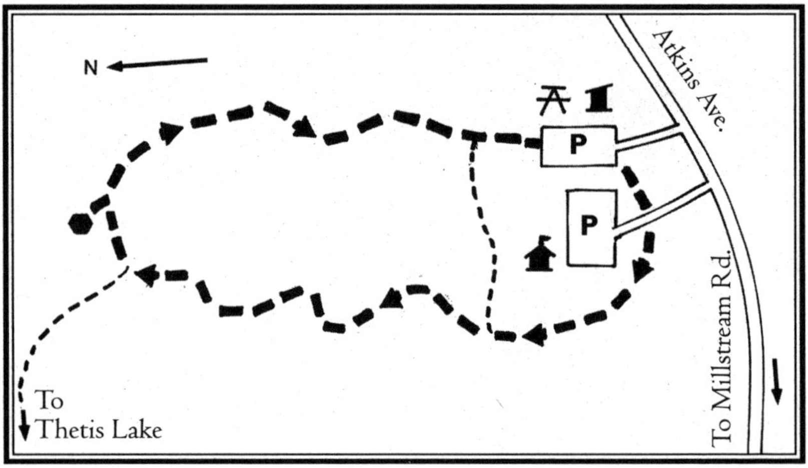

April, the bent-back or recurved white petals of the flowers show up readily in the grass. The deep bulbs take up to seven years to flower and usually grow in clusters formed as the seeds drop close to the parent flower. You will also see the other wildflowers typically associated with Garry oaks, such as pink satin flowers and magenta-pink shootingstars. It is, of course, wonderful habitat for common and greater camas, which in May turn the grassy slope a rich, violet blue.

In June and July, when most of the wildflowers are either white or yellow, it is a welcome surprise to find Menzies' larkspur blooming in the open meadows and on rocky bluffs. From the 40-cm (16-inch) tall stem of this attractive plant, a close relation of the garden delphinium, hang clusters of flowers that are azure blue to violet. Look closely at one of these flowers; the five large "petals" are actually sepals, or calyx-leaf, the uppermost prolonged backward into a spur. In the spur are two nectar-bearing petals, which form a second spur within the first, ensuring that only the long proboscis of a bumblebee or butterfly can reach the deep nectar.

When the switchbacks come to an end, you will cross a rock face and arrive at the most challenging section of the trail. Once you have manoeuvred over the rock face, a compact trail will lead you to a large boulder. The roughly parallel striations, deeply scored into the surface during the last glaciation of the area 25,000 years ago, and the liberal covering of yellow-flowering stonecrop make this rock worthy of attention. Past the boulder you will have to pull yourself up by using footholds in the rock. This viewpoint rewards you with a view of the Olympic Mountains and Juan de Fuca Strait as well as the Sooke Hills and the north Saanich Peninsula. At this lookout there is a good stand of hairy manzanita, the heather shrub that looks so like a dwarf arbutus.

This viewpoint is not the top of the hill, and about 200 m (650 feet) beyond it is a sign marking the Summit trail. Take this short path, which will take you right to the top, where the 360-degree views are breathtaking. To the east you can see Esquimalt Harbour in the foreground, with Victoria behind. The concrete foundations at the summit, all that remains of a forestry station, make a good platform to rest and recover your breath while you watch for turkey vultures and other raptors. There is something wonderful about being at the top of a precipice. You can almost imagine how a soaring bird must feel as it hangs, far above everything else.

To pick up the trail, retrace your steps to the Summit trail signpost. From there go left, and continue along the Calypso trail until you reach another sign marking the route to Thetis Lake. This is a connector trail that has been developed to link Mill Hill Park with Thetis Lake Park. Take the trail to the right, which leads downhill. You are now on Summit trail, which winds down the hill, alternating between open clearings and rich forest. The trees on this side of the hill are larger, their size and wide-spreading canopies giving the impression of adequate moisture even during a hot, dry summer. From the trail the views are toward Victoria, and on a clear day it is worth stopping to look. Partway down the hill the trail becomes difficult, with loose stones and a rock face to clamber over. Take care, as this will be slippery in the wet months of winter and spring.

Before it reaches the bottom, the trail weaves through a mixed forest of large maples, Douglas-firs and grand firs. You will come to a sign marking the conjunction of the Calypso, Summit and Auburn trails. Take the Auburn trail and continue down to the parking lot.

HOW TO GET THERE: Mill Hill Park is located on Atkins Avenue. Take Highway 1 west to Millstream Road. Turn left on Millstream Road and left again on Atkins. The park is about 1 km (½ mile) down Atkins and is well marked.

22

Glen Gardens and Trail

ROYAL ROADS UNIVERSITY
COLWOOD

HIGHLIGHTS: Rain forest, skunk cabbage, tree frogs, birdwatching

WALKING LEVEL: Moderate

SEASON: All year

ATTIRE: Rainwear in winter and sturdy walking shoes

DOG WALKING: Dogs must be on a leash at all times

ROUND TRIP: 1.5 km (1 mile)

IN THE HEART OF Colwood, just outside Victoria, is a little-known and delightful walk called Glen Gardens and Trail. There you may meander through a woodland ravine on the grounds of Royal Roads University, formerly the estate of James Dunsmuir. Royal Roads, or Hatley Park, as it was originally known, is famous for its magnificently landscaped gardens but much less well known for the beauty of its natural West Coast backdrop. The estate was completed in 1908 after two and a half years of construction at a cost of $4 million. Formal gardens, created around a series of small lakes and ponds, covered approximately 160 of the 263 ha (400 of the 660 acres) and employed over a hundred gardeners. In 1940 Hatley Park was purchased by the federal government and became the home of Royal Roads Military College. It remained a military academy until 1996, when the University of Victoria took over the property.

From the parking lot walk down toward Hatley Castle, past the Grant Building, to the intersection of College Road and Cottonwood Creek

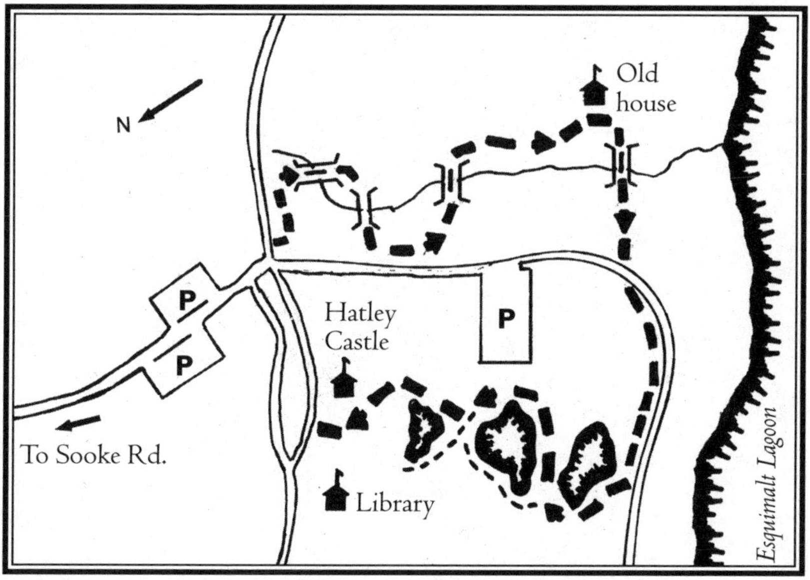

Road. Look for a wooden sign on the left-hand side of the road that reads "Glen Gardens and Trail." Other landmarks to watch for are a wooden bench and a giant sequoia. Sequoias are the acknowledged giants of the forest, and this one, a seedling from King's Canyon in California, is spectacular. About 15 m (50 feet) past this tree, stone steps lead down past a Douglas-fir, also of impressive size. The Douglas-fir is the largest native tree species in Canada, and some first-growth Douglas-firs are almost as large as the sequoias. Its scientific name, *Pseudotsuga menziesii,* commemorates Archibald Menzies (1754–1842), who collected the first specimens of the tree while serving as naturalist with Captain George Vancouver's expedition to the coast in 1792.

As you make your way down the path, the trail winds around an extensive rockery and gradually will take you across a water sluice and to the bottom of the ravine. Take a moment to look across at the rockery. Although many exotic species have been planted here, a few native plants such as Oregon grape grow here too, and the expanse of the rockery is remarkable. About 70 m (230 feet) from the start of the path a short boardwalk covers a wet, slippery section of the trail, and after a further 25 m (80 feet) you will come to a wooden bridge spanning Cottonwood Creek,

Colwood Creek

a small stream that runs the length of the walk. Walk carefully on this section of the trail because it has many uneven and slippery rocks and stones.

You have now reached the forest floor, and the path gradually becomes easier. This is a dark, dank, typical West Coast forest. Coniferous trees predominate here because the area's rainfall occurs mostly between November and March, when the deciduous species are dormant. Western red cedars stand interspersed with Douglas-firs and an occasional bigleaf maple. Bitter cherry and ocean spray accompany the trees, and in the dim light of the forest foam flowers, twin flowers and the blooms of coast boykinia glow brightly. The sounds of the tinkling creek form a musical counterpoint to the quietness of the great trees, and the soil has a rich, organic scent. This is a wonderful walk and an experience not to be missed.

The further you walk down the creek bed the wetter the going becomes, and you begin to see pockets of skunk cabbage. This bright yellow-green plant loves a boggy habitat and is easily identified by its large, fan-like leaves, which stand 0.5 m (1½ feet) tall, and by the distinctive sour "skunk" odour it produces to attract pollinating insects. The scent is thought to mimic rotting meat or dung and is apparently irresistible to beetles and flies. The West Coast rain forest is a tough environment, however, and not all plants thrive as well as skunk cabbage. The abundant rainfall leaches valuable nutrients from the soil, and because of the high water table, the trees are shallow-rooted and unstable. About halfway down the trail you see the result of such conditions, two enormous Douglas-fir blowdowns, where the trees' roots have been wrenched from the soil. This species is less tolerant of heavy rainfall than are western red cedar and hemlock, and, as the tipped-up roots of these fallen Douglas-firs testify, it does not take much to bring them down.

Another potential danger to these forest trees is fungi. The honey mushroom is an example of a parasitic fungus that causes root rot and decay in living trees. Attacking weak trees, it spreads to neighbouring trees by means of black, shoestring-like structures called rhizomorphs, which grow underground. Many fungi, however, are more benign companions, living in a natural harmony that benefits both fungus and tree. In this symbiotic relationship, known as mycorrhiza or fungus root, the fungus spreads a mat of fine hair called mycelium through the top layer of soil, just above the tree roots. If the combination of tree and fungus is right, the mycelium will absorb water and minerals and, by doing so, will also benefit the tree. In return, the fungus is provided with sugars produced by the tree through photosynthesis. Foresters believe that without this symbiotic relationship, most of these trees would barely stay alive. Usually this process takes place underground and is not obvious to the passerby. However, look for exposed roots that sometimes display the mantle of mycelium the fungus has woven.

In autumn it is thrilling to come across the many varieties of mushrooms in this forest. Look for the very poisonous but beautiful *Amanita muscaria*, or fly agaric, with its brilliant orange or red cap, white scales and skirt-like ring on the stalk. This species especially likes Douglas-fir and often grows in the ground cover of twin flower at the base of these trees.

Also look for the various species of bracket fungi, such as dryad's saddle. This rust-coloured fungi usually occurs on deciduous trees, dead or alive, and grows in concentric rings. Each year adds another ring to the outer edge of the preceding year's growth.

Further down the trail, as you start to move away from the creek bed, you will pass under a trestle bridge and travel through a cedar forest. The undergrowth is sparse, with only the odd clump of sword ferns, and the forest is dark. A short way down the path is a little brick building bearing a number 29, possibly used for storage in the past. Keep along the main trail and you will find yourself back at the creek bed, where a wooden bridge stands. Cross the bridge and look out toward a vista of cattails, skunk cabbages, horsetails and shrubs of willow and Pacific ninebark. This is a lush area, part swampy woodland, part marsh, as indicated by the plants growing here. Tree frogs croak in the foliage and in summer you may see a family party of tree creepers busily making their way up the trunks of the trees.

The path leaves the creek bed and moves up and out of the ravine, ending a short distance away at a paved road. Directly in front are playing fields, and to your left is Esquimalt Lagoon. Beyond is the stretch of water known as Royal Roads, where Royal Navy ships would anchor, a reminder that at the turn of the century Esquimalt was the principal base for the navy's Pacific fleet.

Continue walking along the paved road at the edge of the lagoon. Here you are likely to see swans or Canada geese paddling among the reeds and grasses, and in winter, a good variety of diving and dabbling ducks as well as shorebirds arrive. Continue to the end of the lagoon, where you can join a trail that leads back to the parking lot through the formal gardens. You will find this path just past the water sluice that runs through the gardens. Watch for the western painted turtles that live in the small lakes of these gardens. Their top shell, or carapace, is dark olive, blotched irregularly with dark brown and bordered by a narrow band of yellow. Their underside, or plastron, is brightly painted in a pattern of red, yellow and black, giving this creature its name. At the top of the gardens you will find yourself back at Hatley Castle, from where it is a short walk back up the hill to the parking lots.

Velvet-top fungus

HOW TO GET THERE: Take Highway 1 west to Highway 1A, turning off at the Colwood exit. Travel west on Highway 1A, just past Colwood Corners (Goldstream Avenue), and look to your left for the main entrance to Royal Roads University. Travel down the paved entrance roads to the parking lots. Parking lots 1 and 2 are for visitors and charge a small hourly fee.

23

Witty's Lagoon Regional Park

METCHOSIN

HIGHLIGHTS: Nature centre, waterfalls, horsetails, lagoon, birdwatching, beachcombing, wildflowers, picnic area

WALKING LEVEL: Easy to moderate; optional wheelchair-accessible route

SEASON: All year

ATTIRE: Warm and waterproof clothes in winter

DOG WALKING: Dogs must be under control; no dogs allowed June 1–September 15

ROUND TRIP: 3 km (2 miles)

WITTY'S LAGOON IS A wonderful regional park lying in the Bilston Creek watershed, about a twenty-minute drive from downtown Victoria. Historically home to the Northern Straits Salish people of the Ka-Kyaakan band, this 56-ha (138-acre) park offers a ramble through woodlands bordering a rich lagoon. Take the park entrance leading to the nature centre, and if it is springtime, enjoy the meadow of camas and nodding onion that greets you just before the parking lot.

Pick up the gravel path just beyond the map and information board, and on your right, note the giant arbutus growing on the bank. As you look around, you will see that the arbutus is not the only large tree in the area; huge Douglas-firs, grand-firs and cedars also grace the entrance to the park. Beyond the arbutus the path descends, taking you down 140 m

(460 feet) to Bilston Creek. Here a boardwalk begins, giving you a choice of two trails: the Lagoon trail and the Beach trail. Although the Lagoon trail is well worth following, this chapter describes the equally fascinating Beach trail.

Proceeding along the boardwalk, you will cross a sturdy bridge over Bilston Creek. Stop on the bridge for a moment and look up the creek to an outcropping of rock, covered in summer by a profusion of pink monkey flowers. From the other side of the bridge, look downstream and you will see Sitting Lady Falls, no more than a trickle in the summer, but in winter a torrent of water tumbling down the volcanic rock. Here mist rising from the falls irrigates the mosses and stonecrop that cling to the bank. Cascades of ocean spray and the moss-covered, gnarled maples add their richness to the green of the water grasses growing in pools among the rocks. The abundance of vegetation and the movement of the water give the scene an ethereal quality.

After leaving the waterfall, go to the end of the boardwalk and pick up a compact dirt trail, which leads toward the lagoon by way of the creek bed. Here you walk under a forest canopy of Douglas-firs, maples and cedars, with an undergrowth of sword ferns and heucheras. Walk quietly and you may come upon a deer, one of the many that inhabit the park.

Approximately 130 m (430 feet) from the bridge, the path descends a set of stairs built into the bank. If the weather is wet, be careful, for there is no handrailing. At the bottom of the stairs you are again in the damp greenery of the creek edge; arbutus trees and birches grow on the opposite bank. Watch for an enormous Douglas-fir that stands about 50 m (165 feet) from the stairs. It is an ancient and magnificent specimen and a reminder that trees of this kind can live over a thousand years.

The path now winds through hedgerows of blackberry and chest-high salmonberry, with avens, fringe cup and small-leaved buttercup below. Throughout this undergrowth there is a mass of horsetail, a certain indication of a damp location. In the Pleistocene age, long before the appearance of more advanced plants, this ancient plant and its close relations once grew in great forests, bequeathing us a legacy of vast coal deposits. "Scouring rush" is another name for it, because its silicone content makes it useful as a pot scrubber. Today, the silicone that comes in handy to campers with burnt frying pans is used to colour fireworks.

The path continues downhill to another set of stairs. This descent is quite steep but short, and the trail soon levels and passes under the arch of an old apple tree, one of the many fruit trees left from John Witty's farm. The track winds through a rich, low-lying area, where narrow tributaries trickling toward the creek wear away the soil and form islands of muddy grasses. This country is perfect for the muskrat—damp and fertile, with good cover of water parsley, buttercups, sorrel, sedges, rushes and grasses. You may catch sight of one, a small dark snout cutting through the water at the apex of a V of ripples.

A boardwalk allows you to travel dry-shod above the wet terrain to the beginnings of a new forest, where spindly Douglas-fir and twisted arbutus rise above wild rose bushes, ocean spray and bracken ferns. This is a drier part of the forest, where the fallen leaves of arbutus rustle underfoot. The path skirts the edge of the water and gives glimpses of the wildlife of the lagoon. Herons stand motionless in midstride, with downward-directed, binocular vision, searching for fish or frogs.

About 150 m (500 feet) into this forest, the trail divides; take the branch closest to the water to get the best views of the lagoon. In spring and summer, at the far side of the lagoon, the flowers of the arbutus throw creamy-white splashes of colour against the dark green of the conifers and give a welcome variety. Later in the year, its reddish berries provide a different colour counterpoint. Watch your step on this section of the trail; where the soil has eroded, exposed tree roots may trip the unsuspecting walker.

A short distance down the path is a small wooden bench nestled against a hedge of sprawling honeysuckle. This is the hairy honeysuckle, and although its purple-pink flowers are not as showy as those of the orange species, they are sweetly scented. Continue along the trail, cross a small wooden bridge and walk along a path bordered by snowberry and wild rose. These tall shrubs are perfect cover for songbirds, some of which may be spotted in any season. Although the migrant warblers and hummingbirds stay only long enough to breed, others, like chestnut-backed chickadees, remain. They sometimes keep company with tiny gold-crowned kinglets, red-breasted nuthatches and creepers. On the water side of the path, trees grow out from the bank and lean toward the lagoon, softening the contours of the shoreline. Out on the water you may

Muskrat habitat at Witty's Lagoon

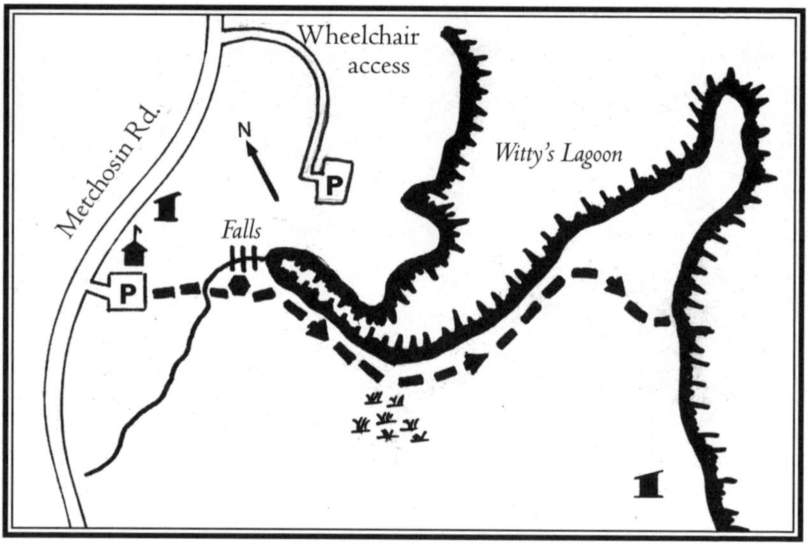

be lucky enough to spot a river otter. They are not uncommon, and the lagoon provides prime otter conditions—good fishing, where salt water and fresh water meet; and overhanging trees with exposed roots, which provide dens for the otters.

The last section of the trail, before it reaches Parry Bay, offers no views of the water; the hedgerows are high, and a canopy of trees gives the path the semblance of a tunnel. In early spring, look for fawn lilies growing in the shrubbery. The high hedgerows soon give way to reveal an open meadow with a spectacular Garry oak on the left. Around the oak, its small companion plants—satin flowers, camas and shooting stars—bloom in the spring. As you pass the giant tree, the first glimpses of the ocean can be had. The path becomes a boardwalk, taking you over a damp area strewn in summer with the flowers of silverweed, vetch and water parsley.

The path ends at the beach, where there are washrooms and a picnic area. If the tide is out, make the short walk along the beach toward the end of the spit. The sand holds many small surprises, if you look carefully. For example, you may detect the small holes of burrowing purple crabs, which inhabit the intertidal zones. If the tide is in, try to spot the harbour seals that come to fish in the shallow waters of Parry Bay. With their large eyes and relatively high nostrils, the seals are able to see and breath without exposing more than the tops of their heads. Watch for passing orcas, or killer whales, the seals' main predator and the terror of all marine mammals. Orcas have voracious appetites, and their sudden appearance offshore causes panic among the seals and a rush for shore. Even here they may not be safe, for the whales have been seen chasing seals onto beaches. Once at the end of the spit you can look down to the end of the lagoon, where the salt-water tides flow in to meet the fresh water of Bilston Creek. If the day is clear, look out to the Race Rocks lighthouse.

On the return trip, retrace your steps until you come to the fork in the trail beyond the Garry oak meadow. It is better to take the inland route rather than the lagoon side, because the forest in this section offers several treasures you will not see elsewhere. There are star flowers and heart-leaf spring beauty to give delicate white blooms in the darkness of the forest. Keep your eyes open for the zebra-patterned leaves (dark green and cream) of the rattlesnake plantain. As you walk on, enjoy the fishnet lichen hanging from the arbutus and maples that line the path. This soon joins the other path and forms the main trail. If you continue climbing, you will reach the parking lot in a few minutes.

For wheelchair users, there is an entrance to Witty's Lagoon on Metchosin Road about 150 m (500 feet) before the nature centre entrance. This road is open from noon to 4 P.M. on Saturdays and Sundays, or by appointment. Call the Capital Regional District at 478-3344 to arrange a special time. A 400-m (1300-foot) road travels down to a spacious parking lot, a picnic area in a tree-surrounded grassy field, and a view of Sitting Lady Falls. From this entrance there is also an approach to the Lagoon trail for wheelchair users.

HOW TO GET THERE: Witty's Lagoon is located off Metchosin Road. Take Highway 1 west to Highway 1A, turning off at the Colwood exit. Travel west on 1A to Sooke Road. Follow Sooke Road to Metchosin Road and turn left. Take Metchosin Road to the main park entrance, where the main parking lot and nature centre are located.

24

Metchosin Wilderness Park

METCHOSIN

HIGHLIGHTS: Cedar forest, fungi, skunk cabbage, sword ferns

WALKING LEVEL: Moderate

SEASON: All year

ATTIRE: Rainwear in wet weather

DOG WALKING: Excellent

ROUND TRIP: 3 km (2 miles)

ABOUT 19 KM (12 MILES) outside of Victoria lies a beautiful but little-known park, Metchosin Wilderness Park. Also known as Clapham Park and Hundred Acre Park, this crown land was leased to Metchosin for ten years under a licence of occupation that expires in the year 2000. Although this park has many trails, some leading up to bluffs overlooking the neighbouring valleys, the walk described in this chapter is a circular route that takes you over the floor of the forest and through deep woods—a perfect walk for a hot day.

From the park entrance, a compact dirt path travels downward through an alder grove for about 100 m (330 feet). As you move closer to the floor of the forest, large western red cedars begin to appear, together with their usual satellite plants—salal, ocean spray and bracken ferns. A ditch runs parallel to the trail on the left-hand side, and during the rainy season it retains much of the runoff. Even on a dry, hot day at the end of summer, enough moisture emanates from this natural reservoir to give at least the illusion of dampness under the tree canopy.

Within about 150 m (500 feet), the trail divides. Stay to the right, following a route that travels in a circle for about 3 km (2 miles) and arrives back at this point. When walking this trail you will notice the predominance of western red cedars, with only the odd Douglas-fir challenging

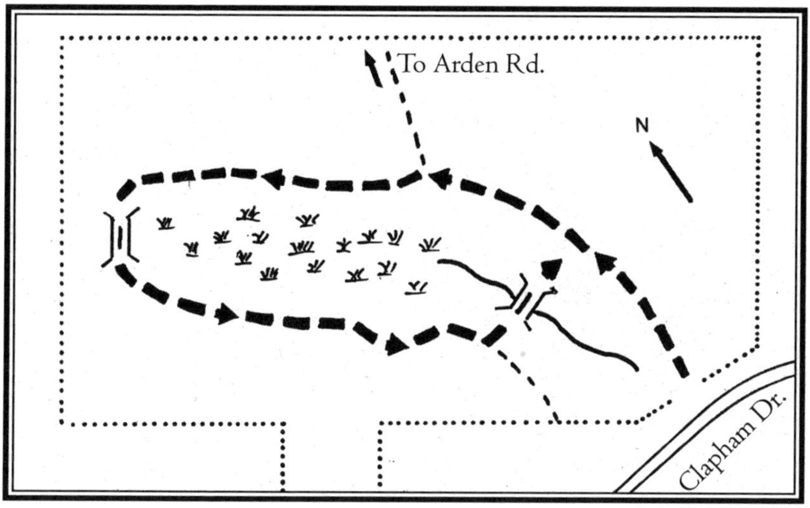

their supremacy. Cedars thrive in these damp conditions, and here on Vancouver Island the heavy rains of winter and spring give them the moisture they need and produce the largest trees. The rot-resistant nature of cedar wood and its ability to split easily made it the cornerstone of northwest coast aboriginal culture. So important has cedar been, both to aboriginal people and to the logging industry, that it has been designated British Columbia's provincial tree. Interestingly, cedars were not felled to any extent prior to the coming of Europeans. The aboriginal people used fallen logs or boards split from standing trees.

As you make your way to the bottom of the forest you will notice clumps of large sword ferns, one of the few plants that thrive in deep shade. Since the cedar canopy prevents much light from filtering down to the forest floor, the sword ferns, with the territory pretty much to themselves, are able to thrive without serious competition. The abundance of these ferns, not to mention their great size, is impressive, and you feel as though you are walking through a sword fern forest. The only other notable plants growing here are pockets of salal and the huckleberry bushes that have taken root in rotting tree stumps.

Take the left fork about 250 m (825 feet) along, where the trail divides again. One of the great pleasures of walking here, further into the forest, is the stillness and the sense of tranquillity. Stop for a moment and listen to the sounds around you. Instead of the roar of automobiles and the grinding of lawn mowers, you will hear branches rubbing together, the wind rustling the trees and the thin notes of birds amplified by the near-silence. Keep an ear open, for many birds in the forest seldom or never show themselves and are only apparent through their calls. Nuthatches and varied thrushes are two such birds, and one that you will undoubtedly hear but probably not see is the tiny winter wren, whose penetrating cascade of song brightens the darkest forest. Even the flamboyant pileated woodpecker, with its ringing cry and scarlet crest, often goes unseen as it flits from tree to tree.

Further down the trail, a large fallen tree is worth examining. Your eye will be caught first by its exposed roots, wrenched free of the soil. This tangle of fibrous fingers had gripped only the surface of the soil, yet the trunk it once supported is massive. How can such a large tree be held by so shallow a root system? Look at the tree from the base to the tip, and you will notice that where its circumference is greatest the bark is just beginning to fall away, while at its thinnest end the tree has decomposed enough to support new plant life.

This part of the walk is a particularly good place to look for fungi in autumn. Oyster mushrooms may be found in overlapping tiers, their white or greyish-brown caps making them "the shellfish of the forest." Look, too, for for the the tiny goblets of the common bird-nest, which feed and grow on rotting wood. This species forms a cylindrical "nest" or cup, which holds what appear to be minute eggs that are attached by tiny cords. As the nest withers the eggs are dispersed, either by drops of rain or by adhering to some transporting agent such as a beetle.

Further down the trail you will come to a marsh, where Pacific ninebark and hardhack form thickets. At the far end of the marsh, skunk cabbage can be found among the rushes, adding a splash of lime green and golden yellow to the otherwise dark forest. Just beyond the marsh, you will cross a wooden bridge that leads to a division in the trail. Stay to your left, because the right side leads out of the park to another parking lot at Arden Road.

The route continues on a drier side of the park, where Douglas-firs are more common. Understorey plants are abundant here, and both salal and Oregon grape grow from the mosses that thickly clothe the forest

Entrance to Metchosin Wilderness Park

floor. About 300 m (1000 feet) from the first bridge, you will come to the second one. Cross it and continue straight on, ignoring the other trails, which lead from the bridge to other sections of the park. The trail takes you down and passes through another swampy region, where a profusion of sword ferns produce an atmosphere of primeval antiquity. You might not wish to linger; mosquitoes love it here.

From the swamp the path leads up to drier land, and alders once again appear, signalling the start of the trail. Soon you will come to the beginning fork, where you bear right and return to the park entrance on Clapham Drive.

HOW TO GET THERE: Metchosin Park is located on Clapham Drive. Take Highway 1 west to Highway 1A, turning off at the Colwood exit. Travel west on 1A to Sooke Road. Follow Sooke Road to Metchosin Road and turn left. Take Metchosin Road to Happy Valley Road. Follow Happy Valley Road to Rocky Point Road. Turn left onto Rocky Point and follow it for about 3.5 km (2 miles) to Clapham Drive. Turn right onto Clapham and follow it almost to the end, where the park entrance is marked with a large wooden sign. There is no parking lot, so choose a safe place at the side of the road to park.

25

Roche Cove and Galloping Goose Trail

ROCHE COVE REGIONAL PARK
MATHESON LAKE REGIONAL PARK
EAST SOOKE

HIGHLIGHTS: Rain forest, salamanders, lake views, picnic area, mud flats

WALKING LEVEL: Moderate; partially wheelchair accessible

SEASON: All year

ATTIRE: Rainwear in autumn and winter

DOG WALKING: Excellent

ROUND TRIP: 3.5 km (2¼ miles)

ABOUT THIRTY YEARS AGO some farsighted city planners in Seattle took an abandoned railway line and transformed it into a walking and cycling trail, now known as the Burke–Kilman trail. This rail-to-trail conversion set a precedent for similar projects all over North America, and Capital Regional District Parks was one of the first to adopt the idea in Canada. In 1987 CRD Parks successfully converted an abandoned Canadian National Railways line into the Galloping Goose trail. The name "Galloping Goose" was originally used by the people of Metchosin and Sooke in the early 1900s to describe the single-car train that serviced their area. The train was famous for bouncing its passengers up, down and sideways. Now extending for a distance of 60 km (38 miles), the trail runs from McKenzie Avenue, through the Selkirk area of Vic West, out to Metchosin and then to Sooke, where it ends at Leechtown, on the

Matheson Lake

Sooke River. This trail is a treasure for cyclists, horseback riders and walkers alike.

The walk described here begins on the Galloping Goose trail in Roche Cove Regional Park but diverts onto a less travelled trail that ultimately leads to Matheson Lake. This secondary path is not an easy walk; for a gentler, less demanding route, stay on the Galloping Goose trail. It also leads to Matheson Lake. Being a former rail line, the Galloping Goose trail is generously wide and the grade is low, not more than 2 percent, making it a consistently easy walk.

Pick up the Galloping Goose trail at the Roche Cove Regional Park parking lot, which has wheelchair-accessible toilets. The trail is bordered by massive, moss-covered rock faces, brightly ornamented in spring and summer with patches of yellow-flowering stonecrop. Salal, with its wiry stems and glossy, ovate leaves, dominates the understorey beneath bigleaf maples, grand firs and Douglas-firs. If you walk here in in late July or August, the vegetation gives off a sweet, dry scent of summer and old leaves crackle underfoot. It is hard to believe that the storms of winter bring as much as 5 m (16 feet) of rainfall to this side of Vancouver Island every year.

Continue down the trail past a "34 km" marker and travel a further 500 m (1650 feet) to the sign for the Roche Cove trail, which at that point joins the trail leading to Matheson Lake. Although it is well maintained, the path is steep and can be slippery during wet weather. Follow it to the bottom at Roche Cove and ignore the Matheson Creek trail for the moment. Although the shoreline is rocky, the beach is a mud flat created by the silty outflow of Matheson Creek. That stream is now a mere trickle, but the flow of water that gave the beach its character was probably much greater prior to the damming of Matheson Lake. Like most mud flats, this one lies in a sheltered spot, protected from the strong currents that would soon carry its sandy sediment out to sea.

At low tide a mud flat seems a barren place, but first appearances can be deceiving. There is life but it is hidden, for the plants and animals that make their homes here are primarily burrowers, living below the surface and out of sight when the flats are exposed. You must look closely for signs of life, such as the castings of the lugworms, who live in U-shaped burrows, or the dark brown or purplish-black mud nemertean making its

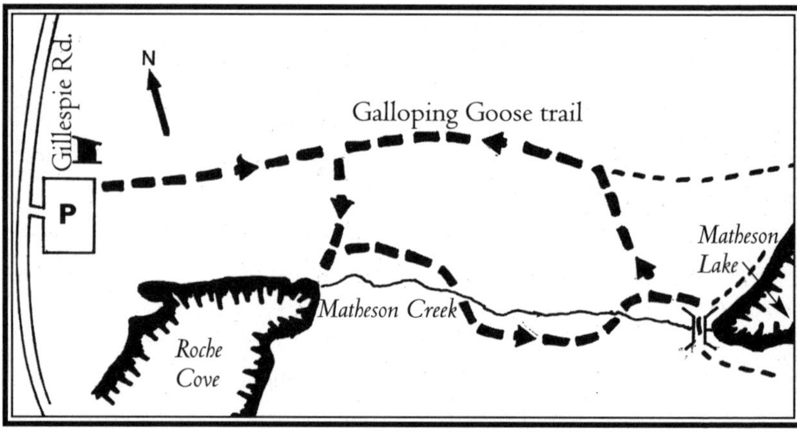

way across the surface on its slime trail. Unlike rocky shores, where there is no shortage of hard surfaces to which an organism can attach itself, a mud flat offers little in the way of an anchorage. Creatures such as the green burrowing anemones must attach themselves to buried shells and become active only at high tide, when the waters bring the small organisms upon which they feed.

Although the sea creatures of this beach are not at first noticeable, they attract a wealth of gulls and other birds to the area. Twice a year, in early spring and late summer, great flocks of shorebirds, which have bred in the high latitudes to the north or wintered in the south, sweep the coast. Almost all the smaller species of waders feed on intertidal marine vertebrates. They congregate in Roche Cove and on similar stretches of shoreline in the thousands. Perhaps the most numerous little sandpipers are the stubby and gregarious dunlins, but among them will be a few teetering, attenuated yellowlegs, some dowitchers with flexible tips to their long bills and perhaps a few sandy-brown, bantam-sized whimbrels, which have deeply curved bills and slender, bluish legs. The most endearing of the confusingly similar horde are the sanderlings, small and noticeably white, who race ahead of the incoming waves on a blur of black legs, searching the tide-wrack and sand for anything edible.

Continuing your walk, travel back up the path from the beach and join the Matheson Creek trail. This narrow track follows the creek bed through a rich, temperate rain forest, characteristic of the coastal western

Roche Cove

hemlock zone. Proximity to the ocean gives this area moderate temperatures all year round and results in cool summers and mild winters. The mild climate, coupled with heavy rainfall, produces large coniferous trees and lush vegetation. The forest plants, however, must rely on nutrients in organic matter, such as humus and rotting wood, because the tremendous amount of rainfall causes a constant leeching of minerals from the soil. Everywhere you look, droplets of water cling to leaves, tree limbs and rotting debris.

About 200 m (650 feet) down the trail, you will come to a shady forest of cedar trees and maples, where sword ferns stand 1.5 m (5 feet) tall. Walk quietly and look carefully among the ferns and rotten wood for a western red-backed salamander, which has a broad reddish or yellowish band running down its back from tip to tail. Although this salamander is a terrestrial amphibian, it depends on moisture for its survival. Look also for the northwestern salamander; with a stouter and much longer body than the western red-backed, it ranges up to 20 cm (8 inches) long. A third species of salamander occasionally seen here is the clouded salamander. The spongy, rotting wood that litters the coastal rain forest is home to this amphibian; remember that a thoughtless footstep or the idle crushing of a decaying log may cause the death of one of these small and fascinating creatures. Another forest dweller to avoid stepping on is the banana slug, one of the few slugs native to the West Coast. This herbivore has a tremendous appetite and feeds on any green leaf in its path, including the very toxic bracken fern, which apparently has no effect on it.

A further 25 m (80 feet) down the trail is a fork, but continue along the path down to the creek, which you can cross by stepping on stones. During the rainy season the creek may be higher and the crossing more difficult. Once you cross the creek watch for the orange markers indicating the trail, because this is not a well-worn path. Look for a large cedar stump beside the path; the cut-out step in the side of the trunk was made by the logger who felled the tree many years ago. Today a new fir tree grows from the centre and derives its nutrients from the decaying wood of the ancient tree. Further along the trail you will reach a grassy passage, where the canopy of conifers is less heavy and where a growth of alders suggests that at some earlier time the forest was cleared. After another 250 m (800 feet), you will again come down to the creek bed and to the kind of swampy habitat perfect for plants like the skunk cabbage.

Heavy rains in winter make the water table in this forest high. Although this produces lush vegetation, it also creates precarious conditions for the large trees, whose shallow roots make them susceptible to the fierce winds that accompany the winter storms. Many are blown down, and not far down the path you will come to such a blowdown. You may have to clamber up and then under to pass it.

About 200 m (650 feet) down the trail you will once again cross the creek, this time using a large log that has been put in place to form a bridge. Once you are across, the going gets a little tough. Watch your footing, and beware of the many exposed roots and slippery rocks. Another 200 m (650 feet) will bring you to the Roche Cove signpost and then to a division in the trail. Stay on the creek-bed track because the other path leads back to the Galloping Goose trail. Soon you will reach a metal bridge over Matheson Creek, and from here you will get the first glimpses of Matheson Lake. This beautiful, 25-ha (62-acre) lake is particularly good for swimming in the summer and has a 3-km (2-mile) walking trail around its perimeter.

If you wish to extend your walk, take the lake trail, which will eventually intersect with the Galloping Goose trail. If you do not, retrace your steps to the Roche Cove signpost and take the inland trail. This path leads along the left-hand side of the lake and gives a lovely view of pond lilies floating on the surface. The trail continues inland and eventually it, too, joins the Galloping Goose trail at a point where a signpost marks the way back to the parking lot. The route back is flat and less interesting than the Matheson Creek trail, but it is certainly less work. It is approximately 1.5 km (1 mile) back to the start, but there is a bench about halfway for those who need a rest.

Once you are back at the parking lot, take the time to cross Gillespie Road and walk down to Kellet Point, about 150 m (500 feet) along a paved road marked by the CRD. This point offers spectacular views of Sooke Basin and the Olympic Mountains beyond and is a wonderful picnic site.

HOW TO GET THERE: Roche Cove Regional Park is located off Gillespie Road. Take Highway 1 west to the Colwood exit and turn onto Highway 1A. Continue past Colwood Corners and bear right onto Highway 14. Continue along Highway 14, past 17 Mile House, and turn left onto Gillespie Road. Three kilometres (2 miles) further will bring you to the park entrance and the parking lot.

Acknowledgements

MY LOVE FOR WALKING in nature began when I was child on the slopes of Mount Tolmie. There, my grandfather and I would spend many a happy hour searching for an elusive lizard or strolling through meadows of camas. My appreciation for the natural world has continued as I have learnt more about the plants, birds and animals around me. For this I owe much to my husband, whose passion for birds has been infectious.

Many people have helped in the making of this book. I owe a debt of gratitude to the patient and helpful people at the Capital Regional District, Russ Dawson at B.C. Parks, and Robert Cannings, curator of entomology at the Royal British Columbia Museum. I am also grateful to Bryce Kendricks for sharing his knowledge of fungi, and to Del Meidenger and Andrew McKinnon of the Research Branch of the Ministry of Forests for their knowledge of and enthusiasm for the plant world. Thanks also go to Dave Fraser, endangered species specialist with the Province of British Columbia, for his constant good humour and patience with all my questions. Finally, I wish to thank my sister, Alison Nicholson, whose knowledge of botany never failed me and whose encouragement was deeply welcomed.

Index